H. Dv. 12:
ARMY RIDING REGULATION 12

GERMAN CAVALRY MANUAL
ON THE TRAINING OF HORSE AND RIDER

BERLIN, August 18, 1937

(LAST EDITION)

With Forewords

By ECKART MEYNERS
And CHRISTOPH HESS

Translated to English

By STEFANIE REINHOLD

© Stefanie Reinhold 2014

 XENOPHON PRESS

Published by Xenophon Press LLC

7518 Bayside Road, Franktown, Virginia 23354-2106, U.S.A.

xenophonpress@gmail.com

ISBN-10   0933316518
ISBN-13   9780933316515

Front cover photographs:

Upper left: Ludwig Stubbendorf on Nurmi at the 1936 Games of the XI Olympiad, Berlin (individual and team gold medal in Eventing).

Lower right: Otto Lörke on Chronist.

Printed in the U.S.A.

Cover design by Naia E. Poyer

1978346

H. Dv. 12

Reitvorschrift

(R. V.)

Vom 18. 8. 1937

Berlin 1937

Verlag von E. S. Mittler & Sohn

Xenophon Press Library

Xenophon Press continues to bring new works to print in the English language such as this translation of a classic work. Xenophon Press is dedicated to the preservation of classical equestrian literature. Available at www.XenophonPress.com

30 Years with Master Nuno Oliveira, Michel Henriquet 2011
A Rider's Survival from Tyranny, Charles de Kunffy 2012
Another Horsemanship, Jean-Claude Racinet 1994
Art of the Lusitano, Yglesias de Oliveira 2012
Baucher and His School, General Decarpentry 2011
Dressage in the French Tradition, Dom Diogo de Bragança 2011
École de Cavalerie Part II, François Robichon de la Guérinière 1992
François Baucher: The Man and His Method, Baucher/Nelson 2013
Gymnastic Exercises for Horses Volume II, Eleanor Russell 2013
H. Dv. 12 Cavalry Manual of Horsemanship, Reinhold 2014
Healing Hands, Dominique Giniaux, DVM 1998
Horse Training: Outdoors and High School, Etienne Beudant 2014
Legacy of Master Nuno Oliveira, Stephanie Millham 2013
Methodical Dressage of the Riding Horse, Faverot de Kerbrech 2010
Racinet Explains Baucher, Jean-Claude Racinet 1997
The Science and Art of Riding with Lightness, Stodulka 2015
The Art of Traditional Dressage, Volume I DVD, de Kunffy 2013
Great Horsewomen of the 19th Century in the Circus, Nelson 2001
The Ethics and Passions of Dressage Expanded Ed., de Kunffy 2013
The Gymnasium of the Horse, Gustav Steinbrecht 2011
The Italian Tradition of Equestrian Art, Tomassini 2014
The Maneige Royal, Antoine de Pluvinel 2010
The Portuguese School of Equestrian Art, de Oliveira/da Costa 2012
The Spanish Riding School & Piaffe and Passage, Decarpentry 2013
Total Horsemanship, Jean-Claude Racinet 1999
Wisdom of Master Nuno Oliveira, Antoine de Coux 2012

Table of Contents

Preface to the English Edition

H. Dv. 12 is somewhat unknown to many English speaking riders yet is well-known in the German speaking riding world. *H. Dv. 12* is a German Army Regulation Riding Provision guiding the instruction of recruits and the training of horses last updated in 1937.

H. Dv. 12 has its roots in the regulations dating back from 1882. These regulations summarized the knowledge gathered together in cavalry training since the 18th century. The riding instructions were revised in 1912 and again in 1926, and were issued as military regulations revised as the 12th version again in 1937. The 1912 edition introduced Riding Provisions that were substantially the work of Gustav Steinbrecht based on the content of his book, *The Gymnasium of the Horse* (Xenophon Press 1994) originally published in 1884.

H. Dv. 12 is the pure directive upon which the classic German *Principles of Riding* were written. *H. Dv. 12* effectively forms a link between 19th and 20th century German Horsemanship methodology. The updated military regulations were issued on August 18, 1937 by the Commander in Chief of the Army at the time, Colonel-General Werner Freiherr von Fritsch and were subsequently enacted.

The German National Equestrian Federation subsequently adopted the *H. Dv. 12* of 1937 and edited and revised the content over the years making updates to make the content relevant to the times. Xenophon Press is pleaseed to offer the careful translation work of Stefanie Reinhold in this first ever, and only English edition. We are most grateful for the excellent line editing work of Stephanie Millham.

The straightforward directives laid out in this manual instructed recruits how to take instruction, teachers how to teach, and the aforementioned how to train their horses irrespective of the discipline for which they were intended. Today's instructors and riders will undoubtedly derive huge benefit from the timeless principles and concepts presented here in this first ever English edition.

Richard F. Williams
Publisher
Xenophon Press

Foreword by Eckart Meyners

From the perspective rider/seat education:

Today's FN Guidelines—the Principles of Riding, the official instruction manual of the German National Equestrian Federation—were developed on the basis of the *H. Dv. 12*, whereby the 1937 edition provided the main orientation. The *H. Dv. 12* was developed out of the context of utilization of the military horse. The goal of these regulations was to provide a "user manual" that was guided by the nature of the horse and related to the necessities of military service. The central system of these regulations is the training scale for the horse that is still applicable in all riding theories today. Unlike in the past, today the horse is used for sports and a large percentage of horses—more than 90%—serve recreational riders.

Why is this system necessary?

The horse does not require the system of the training scale for himself, since he naturally masters all abilities contained therein on his own. Just observe a stallion, who is led to a mare in heat: He can piaffe and passage beautifully. Horses are therefore able to execute high-level movements naturally on their own, without the rider.

The presence of the rider interferes with the horse's nature, since the horse was not really meant to be ridden. In this situation it becomes necessary to rebuild the horse's naturalness on a secondary level in order to maintain its soundness and performance ability as long as possible and enable it to enjoy the combined activities with his rider. This requires the *riding theory—the principles of riding*—with its training scale.

As a kinesiology scientist—I am not a riding instructor—I am not really authorized to judge the value of the *riding theory*. After more than 40 years of scientific research on the topic of riding instruction, however, I have found that the training scale is the best kinematics system for the horse. However, this riding theory can only be transferred correctly to the horse, if the rider is also able to be on par with the horse's naturalness. Therefore I would like to evaluate this old equine kinematics system by means of the included interpretation of the rider's seat, in order to determine, whether both systems correspond with one another in terms of their naturalness.

I have been working with the topic of the rider's seat for decades and have made some surprising discoveries in dealing with the subject of *H. Dv. 12* of 1912, of 1926, and of 1937. I would like to summarize this as follows: In 'the old days' the instructors had a sort of 'intuitive knowledge' that is today increasingly replaced by 'knowledge of riding theory.' Both paths lead to the nature of rider and horse, but via a different approach.

In the H. Dv., the seat is not described as a 'form' but instead as a 'posture.' The term 'posture' sets itself apart from the purely physical observation of body parts. We can still observe around the world today that during instruction the rider is pressed into a form instead of being enabled to gain function by handling his own body in order to answer to the horse's movement. The rider's inner attitude alone is reflected in his natural posture on the horse which is then, in turn, reflected in the naturalness of the horse through rhythm and suppleness. These and other interdependencies of the seat were described at the beginning of the 20th century. Today, these can be scientifically proven. They show that an empirical science approach is no less important than classical methods of specific scientific branches.

Here some aspects as examples:

There is a special emphasis on the rider's relaxed buttock muscles so that a horse can move his back without restrictions.

Incorrect hand positions and/or actions and their causes are also identified. It is described how clamping the elbows tight against the body results in raised shoulders and stiff hands.

The relationship between cause and effect is illustrated by describing the leg and foot position. While instructors still today teach students to turn the tips of their feet towards the horse, the authors of the *H.*

Dv. 12 recognized already that this leads the rider's body to stiffen and automatically leads to a stiff horse.

The stirrup length and its positive function was also already recognized, even though we see dressage riders all around the globe today—up to the highest levels—who ride with excessively long stirrups. The authors of the *H. Dv. 12* had already discovered (in 1937 and earlier) that adjusting the stirrups too long made it difficult for riders to maintain the seat and use the legs correctly.

The kinesthetic principle of "function before form"—which is, unfortunately, still not globally implemented today—is realized in the *H. Dv. 12*, where it is phrased as follows: "Total suppleness first—then military form."

I could expand the realizations gained through "intuitive knowledge" by many additional aspects. My key point, however is that the instructors and riders at the beginning of the last century had know-how that was gained by incredibly sensitive feel. Unfortunately, today this knowledge seems to have been lost on the level of practical application.

I hope that more people will seek guidance in traditional riding instruction books such as the *H. Dv. 12*. In this book, they can learn sensible experiences that document that one must see the horse more from the viewpoint of the horse in order to do the horse's nature justice, instead of understanding riding primarily as a mechanical process.

—Eckart Meyners

Eckart Meyners is the author of *Effective Teaching and Riding: Exploring Balance and Motion; Rider Fitness: Body and Brain; Fit for Riding,* and *Rider + Horse = 1,* and more. He has worked with the German National Federation to develop curricula for professional and amateur riders, trainers, instructors, and judges. He is a trainer for the German Equestrian Federation and was a lecturer in physical education at the University of Luneburg in Germany. He regularly conducts clinics in the United States.

Foreword by Christoph Hess

The *H. Dv. 12* is—so to speak—the bible of classical equestrian sports. It is the foundation needed by every rider interested in systematic schooling for himself and for his horse. I am absolutely certain that the reader will find the *H. Dv. 12* to be a great inexhaustible treasure!

The first edition of the *H. Dv. 12* was published in 1912. In 1937, it was substantially revised. After World War II, the teachings of the *H. Dv. 12* served as the basis for the "Principles of Riding and Driving" of the German National Equestrian Federation (FN). These principles have been updated on a regular basis. Their language and format are constantly aligned with the changing environment. One hundred years ago, the army schooled exclusively male riders, whereas today's riders are mainly women and girls. This change, combined with the fact that many of today's riders must do without regular instruction and engage in equestrian sports as a recreational activity, was, among other reasons, taken into consideration in the new edition of our principles, which also incorporate new scientific insights.

Nevertheless, the actual core of the content of the German National Equestrian Federation Principles handbook remained as it was recorded in the *H. Dv. 12*. The *H. Dv. 12* is still very much 'up-to-date' —even though it was first published more than 100 years ago.

The *H. Dv. 12* was written in order to systematically organize the schooling of rider and horse in military service. Many times, recruits joined the army, who had never ridden a horse before. This situation created a special challenge for the cavalry's riding instructors. In the *H. Dv. 12* one can read the methods and schooling steps that served as the guideline for educating recruits. This book was of essential importance for the military riding instructors. The individual recruits were required to study the *H. Dv. 12*; because the cavalry did not only provide practical training in the saddle, but also theoretical education—based on the *H. Dv. 12*.

The military purchased young horses that were to be used in case of armed conflict. These horses needed a solid basic education in order to remain (unconditionally!) obedient, even in critical situations on the battlefield. In addition, one already recognized that a systematic basic education of the horse prevented premature wear and tear. The cavalry trained the horses to be well prepared for long distance rides. Horses' well-being was a major priority of the cavalry. A mounted unit was only as good as its horses' preparation for war service. If the horses did not last or could not be ridden by the soldiers as required or desired, this had an immediate effect on victory or defeat on the battlefield. Therefore, health, soundness, and the education of horses was the highest priority.

The *H. Dv. 12* contains instruction on how to school horses of various ages at various levels. One also finds the system that is comparable with today's "training scale." This scale has been included in our *"Principles"* for decades and represents the essential guideline for the education of rider and horse. If schooling occurs along these guidelines, rider and horse will never "get off track." Almost all problems that arise during education can be remedied by diligently and consistently taking the principles of this scale into consideration. The wide-spread implementation of the principles of the *H. Dv. 12* is one pivotal reason that our [German] riders have been so successful in the three Olympic disciplines for decades.

The regulations of the *H. Dv. 12* were created for rider and instructor, irrespective of the equestrian discipline and the goal that the individual rider may pursue. These principles are of interest for any rider—today, as well as 100 years ago.

I hope that you will enjoy reading the *H. Dv. 12*. To expand on this topic, I would like to recommend *The Principles of Riding and Driving*, soon to be available in their latest edition in English.

Christoph Hess
Head of Instruction and Head Members Dept. FN
FEI 4 judge for dressage and eventing, FEI Course Director for rider,
judge, and instructor education

Translator's Introduction

My love of horses always had a theme: Help a horse feel good and perform well. Through somewhat of a winding road, this desire to do right by the horse kept leading me back to the *H. Dv. 12*. During my early riding experiences as a child and teenager in Germany in the 1960's and 1970's I had more than one former cavalry man as a riding instructor. Commands were yelled out with conviction, the well-educated school horse was always right; the students were mostly frightened. The *"Richtlinien"* (guidelines) were often quoted even though neither I, nor any of my peers at the time had ever read them. While apprenticing at a show barn in the 1970's, I first became interested in the *H. Dv. 12* while studying riding theory, anatomy and horse care at the jockey school in Cologne.

Since a growing number of respected German authors (Eckart Meyners, Gerd Heuschmann, Kurt Albrecht von Ziegner, Christoph Hess, and others) are quoting the *H. Dv. 12* in their work—which is largely translated into the English language—it seems there has never been a better time to introduce this historical treasure to the English-speaking reader.

There is no denying that the environment in which this last edition [1937] of the German cavalry training guidelines were put into effect was politically difficult. As a native German, I felt our typical "contact angst" dealing with a topic from that time in German history. During the first round of translation, I therefore almost surgically dissected the *H. Dv. 12* in my process, leaving out as many military references as possible. In the end, the publisher and I decided to include these passages both for the purpose of completeness and historical accuracy.

The wealth of knowledge and experience of the cavalry—an institution forever lost to today's equestrian environment—is unparalleled and simply phenomenal. In modern times, we often forget the magnitude of this institution. During WWI, the Germans had roughly 1.4 million horses involved in the war effort. In World War II, a staggering number of 2.75 million horses...with over 80% of all artillery movement executed by horse. The horse was not a negligible part of warfare, instead, a major pillar of strategic planning.

Precondition for wartime success was to keep the animal that this depended on as sound and reliable as possible. Respecting the nature and the needs of the horse, and its non-negotiable anatomical realities, is at the core of the teaching of the *H. Dv. 12*. The horse, as an integral part of the war machine, had to function with predictable reliability. Without the intention of romanticizing the cavalry, war fare, or the horrors of combat, it is safe to say that the cavalry's goal was to create a remount that was a truly willing and able partner, the 'comrade horse,' whose needs were addressed before the rider's.

Translating the *H. Dv. 12* is a project that grew out of the desire to close the loop for the English speaking reader, who may have read any of the above authors, and make this simple yet profound treasure accessible to anyone, who is really interested in keeping their horse sound. In my equine bodywork practice, while teaching seminars or presenting to audiences at fairs and expositions, I encounter plenty of mysterious unsoundness, puzzled owners, and a confusing variety of so-called training methods. Understanding the nature and needs of the horse and the physical abilities the rider must bring to the forefront is the principle of keeping the horse sound. This is key to making the right choices. The *H. Dv. 12* presents a structured schooling methodology for horse and rider in a clear and concise 'how to' language. The reader will want to follow up by reading today's FN Principles of Riding.

This work has been an incredible educational experience for me. I am grateful to Xenophon Press for providing the publishing opportunity. I am also grateful to all teachers I have encountered in my life for instilling an eternal student attitude in me and especially to my early riding instructors—the red-faced yelling kind—who made it very clear, who this activity is all about: always and foremost about the horse.

Wishing you lots of enjoyment and success with this book and your horse!

—Stefanie Reinhold

Introduction

War requires that the rider securely controls his horse on cross-country rides, and that the horse possesses obedience, agility, and endurance. The goal of schooling rider and horse is to fulfill this requirement. Lasting success can only be achieved, if the heart and soul of all superiors and subordinates [instructors and pupils] is filled with the joy of riding and the love of the horse.

The commanders of squadrons etc. are responsible for the uniform education of all riders and horses in the squadron etc., for ensuring that the horse material is maintained in good condition in the long term and for the development of riding instructors. The regiment, detachment, and batallion commanders are responsible for the officers' riding education and supervise the riding education in squadrons, etc.

The level of riding education is tested during inspections. The main purpose of these inspections is to determine whether the end goal of schooling, meaning mastery of the horse cross-country, has been achieved. Such tests will be complemented by comparing the scores of the presented riders and horses with their strengths.

One can also gain an insight into the level of riding education by means of strenuous efforts. The effect of schooling must be that the number of temporarily sidelined horses remains small.

Part A.

I. General Remarks.

1. Schooling Location.

Riding instruction is conducted in the outdoor arena, cross-country, and in the indoor riding school.

During the course of the entire education, instruction in the school or in the arena and cross-country must complement each other.

Riding instruction for all detachments must be moved to the cross-country course as often as possible. This is where rider and horse are schooled in long lines and moving across uneven ground. This type of instruction is especially important for recruits and horses. In open terrain, it is also possible to combine other duties with riding. This provides the opportunity to have all squadrons go out at the same time, which saves time.

2. The Riding Instructor.

The **riding instructor** must not only master his task in theory, but also in practical application. Instructors of remount detachments must themselves have ridden young horses.

The riding instructor must attend to the following points:

Each lesson must be based upon a **time schedule** that was devised ahead of time. During the individual lessons, the sequence of exercises must be conducted appropriately and progress from easier to more difficult exercises.

Schooling plans provided in the sections "Young Remounts," "Horses in the second Year," and "Recruits" provide a guideline for additional time schedules each riding instructor must create.

Whenever difficulties in schooling [dressage] arise, the riding instructor will frequently find cause to consciously deviate from the planned structure of the riding lesson.

Therefore it is necessary to conduct the work in a thorough and slowly progressing manner. It is incorrect, however, not to proceed until the accomplishment completely fulfills all requirements. One must take into consideration that the later exercises will also continue to improve the previous ones.

Suppleness in rider and horse is the most important aspect of the work. Collected exercises may only be conducted after suppleness is achieved.

Stringing together many difficult exercises causes the rider to become stiff and to sit tight. This will cause the horse's gaits to lose impulsion. Especially for recruits [new riders] and young horses, it is necessary to work for only short periods of time, frequently lead the horse and dismount in order to prevent rider and horse from damage.

Riders tend to move about in short gaits that lack impulsion and only ride exercises that are most comfortable to them, but present little challenge to the horse. This tendency must be counteracted.

Frequent breaks—especially after difficult exercises and towards the end of the lesson—serve to provide rest for the horses. During these breaks, the horses must be put on a completely long rein [on the buckle].

During riding instruction, only short 'keyword type' **commands** are appropriate. Longer lectures belong in the [theoretical] instruction, which can occasionally occur in the indoor riding school with the aid of a saddled and bridled horse. If—as an exception—longer explanations are needed during the riding instruction, the instructor asks the participants to halt or gathers his students—mounted or dismounted—around him.

A fresh, varied **teaching style** that avoids predefined patterns creates alert, proactive and passionate students, a precondition for successful instruction. Overly loud commands and too much talking dull the students. Praise and recognition often further the education more than criticism.

The riding instructor also acts as an **educator.** He frequently checks the rider's attire, appearance, and cleanliness of the horses as well as of saddles and bridles. In his students, the riding instructor must develop a feeling for the horse and for its characteristics. He must be focused on having the riders maintain military posture, without ever losing sight of the goal to educate them to the level of complete suppleness.

The riding instructor chooses his **position** in a way (see figure 1) that will also allow him to view the riders from the front and the back, not only from the side. From the front and back he can best observe the

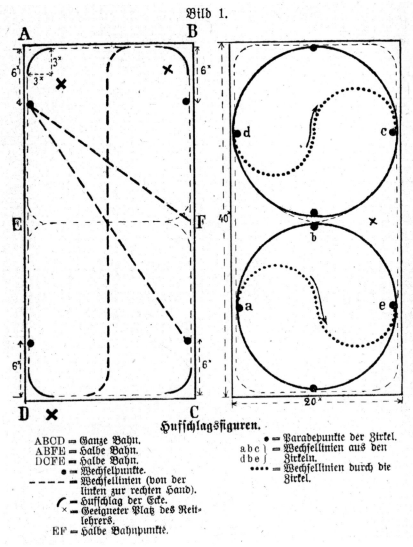

Bild 1.

ABCD = Ganze Bahn.
ABFE = Halbe Bahn.
DCFE = Halbe Bahn.
● = Wechselpunkte.
- - - - = Wechsellinien (von der linken zur rechten Hand).
⌒ = Hufschlag der Ecke.
× = Geeigneter Platz des Reitlehrers.
EF = Halbe Bahnpunkte.

Hufschlagsfiguren.

● = Paradepunkte der Zirkel.
abc / dbe = Wechsellinien aus den Zirkeln.
•••• = Wechsellinien durch die Zirkel.

Figure 1a. School figures.

ABCD - To go large

ABFE - Without change of rein

DCFE - Without change of rein

● – Circle points

- - - Change of rein lines (from the left to the right rein)

Corner track: there is a 'bow' to indicate the corner.

X – Suitable position for the riding instructor

EF - Circle points on "center circle"

● – Halt points of the circles

abc and dbe = change rein out of the circle

...... – Change rein through the circle

5

horse's foot placement and the posture of the rider's upper body. In the riding school, he therefore usually stands at the short wall or—when riding on circles—at the middle of the long wall. When in open terrain and on foot, he chooses his position so that he can reach the riders with his voice.

If he himself rides cross-country with them, he mostly rides behind, less often in front of his group of riders.

(Noch Bild 1.)

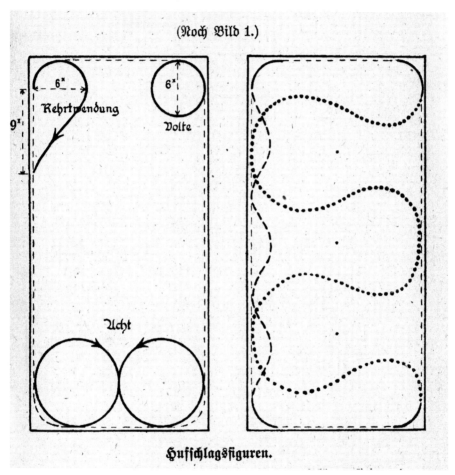

Hufschlagsfiguren.

Figure 1b.

School figures.
----- - Serpentine on the long side
.... – Loop serpentine across the width of the school.

6

At the beginning of an inspection, the riding instructor stands one step off to the right side of the detachment in line with the riders. He commands the move off in front of the middle of the detachment, facing the detachment. Otherwise the riding instructor stays near the inspecting superior. After completed inspection, he resumes his place on the right side of the mustered detachment.

3. Designations.

The **base line** is a line that is imagined to run through the front hooves of a correctly positioned horse of the rider in the middle [of the detachment].

Distance is the space from one horse's tail to the head of the following horse. The distances are measured in steps (80 cm.) and in horse lengths (3 steps).

Interspace is the distance between the sides of two riders standing next to each other, measured from stirrup to stirrup.

When the detachment is lined up, riders keep 3 steps interspace. Deviations must be expressly ordered.

The riders have contact when their stirrups touch.

The necessary level of alignment to the side results from correct alignment of the horses with the base line.

Contact and alignment must be assumed by each rider without special request.

The rider rides on the right (left) rein, when the right (left) rein faces the inside of the riding school (arena).

When the horse is aligned straight ahead, the **inside or inner side** of the horse is the side that faces towards the inside of the school. Otherwise, it is the side towards which the horse is flexed; the **outer side or outside** is the opposite side.

Half-halts are rider influences that prompt the horse to either restrain itself, collect or slow down the speed for the moment, or to transition into a shorter gait.

Full halts prompt the moving horse to halt.

Tempo means the speed in which the horse covers a specific

distance in a specific gait.

The steady sequence and consistent length of the horse's steps and strides within a certain gait is called rhythm.

4. Riding Independently in a Group, Riding Individually.

Riding independently in a group is the rule during riding instruction. It enables the riding instructor as well as the rider to select the gaits, exercises, and speeds that are most suitable for a specific purpose and at a specific point in time. This type of instruction must always be used to initially achieve suppleness and learn new exercises.

For this purpose, the riding instructor gives the detachment or individual riders the order to proceed in a specific gait, tempo or with a specific exercise. He uses voice commands, which may include those listed in the table of commands (subparagraph 8).

Furthermore, he prescribes the rein to ride on. When riding in circles, riders on each circle usually ride on opposite reins.

When riding independently in a group, the riding instructor can also temporarily demand that distances [between horses] be kept. It has the advantage—compared to riding in a detachment—that riders stay mobile, which decreases the risk of developing stiffness. It also provides the opportunity to single out individual horses that are not ready to be ridden in a detachment.

During independent riding in a group, the rider must observe the following arena rules: When halting or moving at the walk, the rider must vacate the track. Evade other riders by moving to the right, do not cut off others when passing them.

When riding individually, each rider can either chose a sequence of exercises or they are prescribed by the riding instructor. If using the former method, the rider is educated to think as a rider. The latter method challenges the horse to a greater level of compliance. This challenge is especially great if most of the other horses are standing together at another place. Therefore, such greater challenges are not appropriate in cases where—due to lack of schooling of horse and rider—there is a risk that the rider will be tempted to overcome the horse's herd instinct and ride many turns by excessive and therefore inappropriate use of the reins. Exercises meant to educate horse and rider to be independent, on the other hand, such as riding away from the detachment and towards certain points, in open terrain also transitioning down to a slower gait and stopping while the herd leaves, must be practiced continuously during individual riding in all detachments (also see subparagraph 44).

5. Schooling as a Detachment. Commands.

Precondition for riding as a detachment following commands is the horses' suppleness as well as that horse and rider equally master the commanded exercises. This ability was achieved by previous individual schooling. Riding as a detachment requires exact adherence to predefined distances and speeds, solidifies the rider's discipline and is a touchstone for the uniformity of the schooling level, is suitable for presentation and serves as preparation for formation schooling. Riding of especially long and difficult exercises as a detachment has a harmful effect on the suppleness of rider and horse. One must therefore refrain from doing so.

The detachment is lined up with its front facing the long side of the arena. The horses' heads remain behind the center line of the rectangle. The center rider stops on the track of the E-F line, All horses stand perpendicular to the base line. The detachment dismounts and the rider corrects the position of its horse as required for presentation (subparagraph 7). The riding instructor first checks the lineup of his detachment from the front, in order to ensure that the main requirement—horses perpendicular to the base line and correct interspaces between riders—is fulfilled. Then he checks the lateral alignment.

Command	Purpose & Execution
Mount! Dismount!	While at ease. Execution see subparagraph 8.
Reins into the left hand!	With snaffle bridle to check the self-carriage.
3-1 rein hold! **Military rein hold!**	Execution see subparagraph 13.

Command	Purpose & Execution
Post the trot! Sit the trot!	Execution see subparagraph 17 & 18.
Detachment (etc.) break out right (left) — march!	The first rider on the right (left) wing moves off in the walk and rides forward straight ahead; all the other riders, one after the other, do the same as soon as the rider to their right (left) has moved past the head of his horse by one horse length; all riders look straight ahead. Three steps before the track, each rider turns right (left) in a quarter-volte and follows the rider in front of him. Each rider then rides with a distance of two horse lengths.
First rider turns right (left), all deploy left (right) — march!	Purpose: Deployment to form a detachment with distances of 3 steps. Shorter or longer distances must be especially specified in the announcing command (for example "with distances of X steps" or "without distances"). Execution: Upon the command of March!, the first rider turns into the arena and rides perpendicular towards the opposite side. The following riders each ride one generous horse length beyond the point where the rider in front of him turned into the arena, and then proceeds in the same way. Upon: First rider - halt! the first rider halts his horse and positions it perpendicular to the opposite side. The remaining riders keep riding at the same speed until they reach the croup of the horse to their right (left) and then move forward into that direction, transitioning from the trot or canter into the walk.

Command	Purpose & Execution
On the right (left) rein, break out right (left), form a detachment — gait!	Purpose: Forming a detachment after riding independently in a group.
Detachment gather behind me (with interspaces of x steps) — gait!	Purpose: Mustering up. The first rider behind the riding instructor determines the direction. The other riders equally deploy on the right and left side with interspaces of three steps, unless commanded otherwise.
First rider traverse to the right (left) — march! **Ride on the [rectangular] track!**	Purpose: The riding instructor uses this command to guide the first rider to the desired track.
B-X-E without change of rein!	Transition to B-X-E without change of rein.
Go large!	Transition to 'go large.'
Ride on the circle!	At the next circle point, the rider transitions onto the circle line, the following riders do the same at the same spot.
Ride on two circles!	Here one must determine who will be the first rider for the second circle.
Advance to a distance of (x) steps — gait! **First rider halt (walk, trot)!**	Execution: If the first rider is to maintain the gait (tempo), the other riders advance in the next higher gait (tempo). If he is supposed to halt or slow down the gait (tempo), the instructor uses this command.

Command	Purpose & Execution
Create distances forward of (x) steps — gait!	Execution: Creating distances forward is always done by going in the next higher gait (tempo).
Change of rein along the long (short) diagonal!	This command is given right before the first rider arrives at the corner on the short side. When cantering, the change of rein is ridden only in shortened working tempo.
Change of rein down the center line!	This command is given when the first rider approaches the second corner on the long side.
Change of rein out of the circle(s)!	Starting with the first rider, each rider transitions to the circle line of the other circle at the circle point on the open side. If riders are riding on two circles at the same time, the riders evade each other on the ride side when riding on the right rein, and on the left side when riding on the left rein.
Change of rein through the circle(s)!	Beginning with the first rider, the riders turn into the circle from the circle point on the open side.
Tighten / enlarge the circle!	Execution see subparagraph 23.

Command	Purpose & Execution
Tighten / enlarge the rectangle!	Execution see subparagraph 32
First rider serpentine on the long side! **First rider serpentine across the width of the school!**	The commands are given before the first corner of the long side. The first rider begins the serpentine after riding through this corner. This exercise can be ridden with and without changing flexion. Flexion is changed when entering each new loop. The number of loops depends on the size of the arena and the schooling levels of rider and horse (see subparagraph 25).
Volte — march!	Execution: Upon 'march!', the rider turns his horse from the track into the volte and returns to the track at the point where he first turned into the volte.
Detachment turn [180 degrees] — march!	Each rider turns on a half volte into the arena and then rides back to a point on the track, that is three or—depending on the diameter of the volte—more horse lengths before the starting point of the turn [volte-face, 180 degrees]. The execution command in the detachment is given in such fashion that the first rider can ride the volte or [180 degree] turn in the first corner of the short side. Voltes and [180 degree] turns are only ridden in the walk. (see subparagraph 24)

Command	Purpose & Execution
First rider [180 degree turn] volte-face out of the corner!	The volte-face is executed by the first rider. The command is given before the first corner of the short side. (see subparagraph 24)
Bend the horses right (left)!	See subparagraph 30.
Flex the horses right (left)!	One starts riding in flexion (see subparagraph 33).
Without changing flexion!	The command is given before the commands for changing to the other rein. The current flexion is maintained on the new rein and one therefore rides with flexion to the outside. As a command for counter canter with individual horses (see subparagraph 19).

Command	Purpose & Execution
Straighten the horses!	Ends the riding in flexion (with bend).
Right (left) flank [90 degree turn] (or about face [180 degree turn]) — march!	Turns during movement (see subparagraph 21).
On the forehand right (left) face [90 degree turn] (or about face [180 degree turn]) — march!	Turn on the forehand (see subparagraph 20).
Right (left) face [90 degree turn] — march!	Turn on the haunches (see subparagraph 20).
Half-pirouette in the walk — march!	See subparagraph 26.
Let the horses yield to the right (left) leg!	See subparagraph 31.
Shoulder-in — march!	See subparagraph 34.
First rider shoulder-in!	
Straight ahead! **First rider straight ahead!**	Ends leg-yielding and shoulder-in.

Command	Purpose & Execution
Detachment (etc.) — halt!	Transition from movement to the halt, full halt (see subparagraph 27).
Detachment (etc.) — march! (from the halt)	Transition from the halt to the walk. 125 x per minute.
Detachment — walk! (from a higher gait)	
Detachment in working tempo — trot! Detachment in working tempo canter — march! (from another gait and from the halt)	Working tempos for example alternating with freer tempos in those detachments that are not allowed to go at a shortened working trot and shortened working canter (young remounts and recruits)
Detachment in shortened working tempo — trot!	Shortened working tempos alternating with freer tempos for detachments, where this is intended according to schedule. The shortness [slowness] of the tempo is determined by the horse that has the least ability to collect of all horses in the detachment.
Working trot!	

Command	Purpose & Execution
Working canter! (from shortened working tempos)	
In shortened working tempo! (from the working and medium trot or working and medium canter)	
Detachment — medium trot! (from another gait and the halt)	Medium trot = 300 x per minute.
Medium trot! (from the working and shortened working trot)	
Extend! (from the medium trot)	Extended trot only with individual horses (see subparagraph 75, last section)
Shorter! (from the extended trot)	Medium trot
Medium canter! (from the working and shortened working canter)	Medium canter = 350 x per minute.
In working tempo! (from the medium trot and the medium canter)	Working trot and working canter.

Command	Purpose & Execution
Squadron, battery, platoon, gun, etc. — trot! (from another gait and from the halt)	Working tempo: 275 x per minute. Rising trot without special command.
Squadron etc. canter — march! (from another gait and the halt)	Working tempo: 500 x per minute (exceptions see subparagraph 56).
Extend! (from the working canter)	Extended canter is only ridden in open terrain. The tempo depends on the position and type of terrain. It is about 700 x per minute.
Shorter! (from the extended canter)	Working canter.
Detachment (etc.) x rein-back x steps — march! Halt! (or gait)	Execution see subparagraph 28.
Sit still!	The rider puts his horse on the bit and assumes the prescribed posture. The rider is permitted to carry out movements that are required to correctly influence the horse.

Command	Purpose & Execution
Line yourselves up!	All riders, with the exception of the first rider on the right wing, turn their eyes to the right and improve the alignment by moving the horse forward or back. If the interspaces must be improved, this occurs by several turns on the forehand and haunches in succession (see subparagraph 20).
Move yourselves!	The rider stays in an erect seat position but is allowed to move freely. In the process, the horse is: in the halt and walk at the long rein or upon command on the buckle, in the trot or canter in the working position.
Sit still! Eyes right! (Eyes left!)	Salute by a halting or marching detachment.
Ending: Eyes straight! Move yourselves!	

6. Saddling and Bridling.

The rider can only properly sit and influence the horse on a correctly built and well-fitting saddle. Good and bad bridling have a considerable effect on the willingness and therefore on the schooling of the horse.

Saddling.

The panels of a well-fitted saddle butt against the horse's shoulder blades and lie flat, evenly against the horse's ribs. The two ends of the panels must be somewhat bent away from the horse's body and their upper edges must not pinch the horse's back anywhere, especially not at the withers. Between pommel and saddle blanket, there must be enough room to reach into with one hand before the saddle blanket is pulled into the gullet.

Fig. 2: Correct saddling.

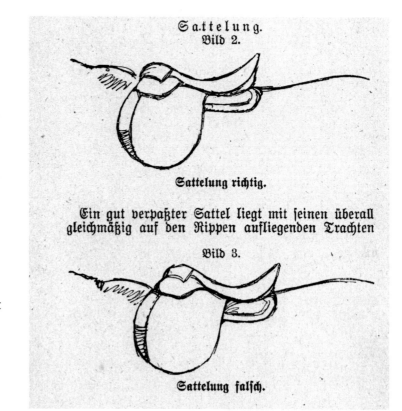

Sattelung.
Bild 2.

Sattelung richtig.

Ein gut verpaßter Sattel liegt mit seinen überall gleichmäßig auf den Rippen aufliegenden Trachten

Bild 3.

Fig. 3: Incorrect saddling.

Sattelung falsch.

The deepest point of the seat must be in the middle of the saddle.[1]

The saddle blanket—folded 6 or 9 times—must be placed upon the horse's back in such fashion, that it protrudes from the front of the saddle by about one hand width and hangs down at equal length on both sides of the withers. The open ends of the saddle blanket must be positioned towards the lower left and the rear.[2]

---

1   [The German Cavalry Saddle — Model M25

As the standard German cavalry saddle from around 1925 through 1945, the 'modern' cavalry saddle M25 was a lightweight, sturdy saddle with a large contact area and plenty of attachment points for various equipment. The saddle weighed about 9.5kg (around 21 lbs) and was based on a wooden tree with a rawhide hammock design as the basis for the seat. This saddle could be completely dismantled and individual parts—such as the seat, for example—could be easily replaced.

The first priority of this saddle design was soundness of the horse over long distances, carrying the weight of rider and equipment. It was certainly not designed with rider comfort in mind. It came in 5 different tree sizes from narrow to draft horse size, also allowing for different back curvature. For the rider, however, one seat size had to do for all. Extremely wide gullets and large contact areas kept pressure off the spine and supraspinous ligaments of the horse and ensured optimal weight distribution. It put the rider close to the horse's center of gravity, but also somewhat suspended above its back. Officers often did not ride as much as the general population of enlisted men and had finer, lighter saddles that were often custom-made.]

2   [The German Cavalry Saddle Blanket

The basic idea of the folded cavalry style saddle blanket—used in similar fashion in the US and French cavalries, for example—is to have an easy-care, multi-functional piece of equipment. First priority was to prevent saddle sores, which would have rendered the horse useless during a campaign. This is achieved by a combination of material and folding technique. The blankets were made of 100% wool, woven in a special twill-weaving technique, similar to denim, and were usually folded into 6 layers. (See separate folding instructions.) Multiple layers break down friction, the number one cause for saddle sores as the movement of the rider and the horse cause friction in the interface between the two bodies: the saddle contact area. Wool wicks away moisture and the blanket dries quickly when unfolded. One can also simply refold and have a dry side against the horse in a minute. The so-called "Woilach" also served as a cooling/warming blanket for the horse.

100% wool, 234cm x 200cm (approximately 92" x 78"), total weight approximately 3.4kg (approximately 7.5 lbs.)

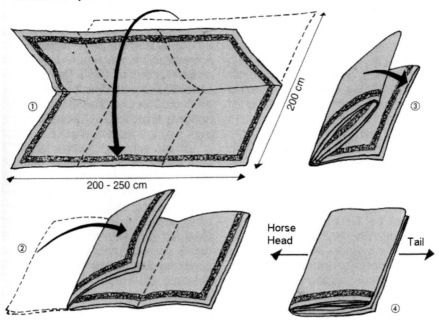

Woilach six layers

① 200 - 250 cm 200 cm ② ③ ④

Horse Head   Tail

[*Editor's note:* The Woilach saddle blanket diagram above, along with its folding instructions as footnote 2 and the description of The German Cavalry Saddle-Model M25 in footnote 1, are inserted here to append this text for the modern reader so as to put into context the equipment being used at the time. These were standard issue pieces of equipment and were 'understood' by riders of the time.]

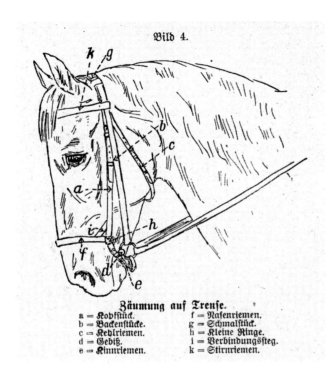

Bild 4.

Figure 4:

The snaffle bridle

a = Head piece
b = Cheek piece
c = Throat latch
d = Bit
e = Chin strap
f = Noseband
g = Crown piece
h = Small rings
i = Connection piece
k = Brow band

Zäumung auf Trenſe.

a = Kopfſtück.   f = Naſenriemen.
b = Backenſtücke.   g = Schmalſtück.
c = Kehlriemen.   h = Kleine Ringe.
d = Gebiß.   i = Verbindungsſteg.
e = Kinnriemen.   k = Stirnriemen.

The snaffle bridle

The bridle must be fitted in such fashion, that the bit (D) touches the corners of the mouth without pulling them up. The crown piece (G) rests on the middle of the poll, the brow band (K) right underneath the ears, comfortably resting against the horse's head; the cheek pieces (B) are about 40 mm. behind the facial crest. The throat latch (C) is adjusted so that the flat hand can be placed between the latch and the throat when the horse yields at the poll.

The head piece (A), the chin strap (E) and the noseband (F) of the bridles are sewn into small rings (H); a small connection piece (I) prevents the noseband from dropping down. This piece must be short enough to allow the two rings to be in front of the bridle's cheek pieces.

The head piece of the cavesson that is to be combined with the bridle is pulled under the bridle's cheek pieces and through the loops of the brow band.

After putting on the bridle, the chin strap is pulled through underneath the snaffle bit and connected with a buckle piece that is sewn into the ring on the left side. The buckle of the buckle piece must be positioned close to the ring. The noseband must be placed about 80 mm above the upper edge of the horse's nostril, the chin strap must be fastened loose enough to allow the horse to chew.

The double bridle

The main piece of the bridle No. 22 [standard cavalry bridle] is positioned far enough behind the horse's ears, so that the cheek piece runs down the horse's cheek at a distance of about 40 mm behind the facial crest. This determines the length of the brow band. The noseband is positioned about 20 mm under the facial crests. The buckle of the throat latch, which must be adjusted to a length that makes it possible to put a flat hand between the latch and the horse's throat when the horse is flexed in the poll, is approximately positioned in the middle of the jowls.

When attaching the curb reins, one must make sure to attach that rein that is 25 mm shorter to the right curb ring.

The **bridoon bit** [snaffle bit] touches the corners of the horse's mouth without pulling them up.

Figure 5:
S-shaped curb bit.

a = Mouthpiece
b = Port
c = Cannons
d = Cap
e = Cheek bar
f = Upper cheek bar
g = Lever arm
h = Rein ring
i = Curb chain hook

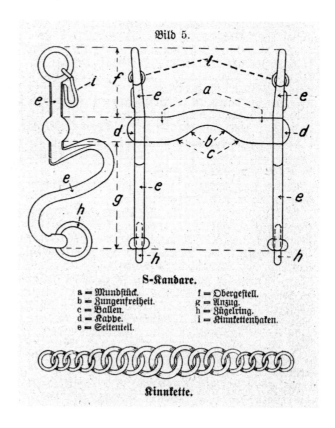

Bild 5.

S-Kandare.

a — Mundstück.
b — Zungenfreiheit.
c — Ballen.
d — Kappe.
e — Seitenteil.

f — Obergestell.
g — Anzug.
h — Zügelring.
i — Kinnkettenhaken.

Curb chain.

Kinnkette.

24

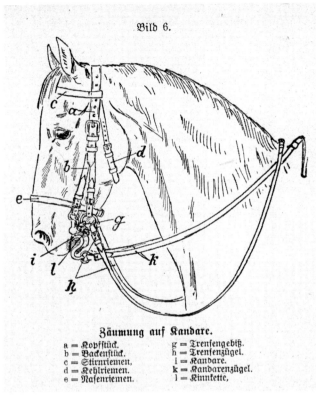

Bild 6.

Figure 6:
The double
bridle

a = Head piece
b = Cheek piece
c = Brow band
d = Throat latch
e = Noseband
g = Bridoon bit
h = Bridoon rein
i = Curb bit
k = Curb reins
l = Curb chain

Zäumung auf Kandare.

a = Kopfstück.   g = Trensengebiß.
b = Backenstück,   h = Trensenzügel.
c = Stirnriemen,   i = Kandare.
d = Kehlriemen.   k = Kandarenzügel.
e = Nasenriemen.   l = Kinnkette,

The **curb bit** must be positioned in the horse's mouth so that the bit is at about the same height as the chin groove and does not touch the canine teeth. For horses that tend to take the nose behind the vertical, the bit is placed a bit higher.

Regarding width, one must ensure to select a mouthpiece that does not show on either side of the horse's mouth; it is equally important to make sure that the upper cheek bars do not press on the lips or the skin of the cheek. Otherwise the curb bit is either "too wide" or "too narrow." The upper cheek bars are always slightly bent towards the outside.

When selecting a mouthpiece, one must pay attention to the question whether the lower jaw is wide or narrow, fleshy or sharp-edged and whether the tongue is thick or thin. For sensitive horses, the best choice is a mouthpiece with a low port, for less sensitive horses one can chose a bit with a higher port.

A mouthpiece with a larger port is also recommended for horses that have the tendency of pushing the tongue above the bit. Mouthpieces with large ports do have the potential of damaging the lower jaw.

The curb chain hooks—bent towards the outside—should reach the mouthpiece. Creating the correct bend of the hooks has a significant effect on proper bridling. Incorrectly bent or twisted or mixed up hooks (e.g. right hook in the left upper cheek piece) leads to injuries to the horse's mouth.

The curb chain must be twisted smooth towards the right side and be positioned in the chin groove, therefore at the same height with the mouthpiece. The last chain link is hooked into the right hook in such fashion that this link stays turned towards the right and the remaining link hangs down on the left side, outside of the hook. Additional overhanging links will be distributed evenly on both sides. In case of an uneven number of links, the majority of links will be on the left side. The curb chain must have no effect until the curb reins are pulled. The curb chain must impact the exact location that is described above as the correct position.

Curb angle

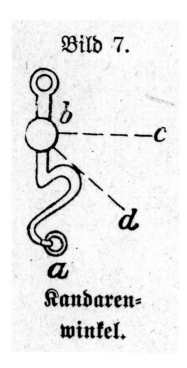

Bild 7.

Kandaren= winkel.

Figure 7.

The lever arms should then be able to go back towards the horse's neck as far as the bisection line b-d of the right angle a-b-c [meaning 45 degrees]. If the lever arms go back behind the b-d line, the curb will not have the desired effect. If the lever arms stay stuck out as an extension of the cheek pieces or if they can only move back slightly, the curb is positioned 'too steeply' and will influence the horse incorrectly (figure 7).

If the bridle is put on correctly, the curb chain will not be pulled up and out of the chin groove when the reins are pulled. The curb chain hooks must remain just about in their position relative to the upper cheek piece. If there is a larger angle between the upper cheek piece and the curb chain hook, the curb chain is too short; in this angle, the lips

26

will be pinched and injured. The curb chain must lie flat against the lower jaw of the horse. This is only possible if the mouthpiece has the right width.

7. Leading Horses in Hand.

With snaffle bridle

The right hand grasps the snaffle reins—which are parted with index and middle finger—one hand width below the rings, so that the right snaffle rein is a bit tighter. The ends of the reins are placed into the full right hand, thumbs on the reins. The rider walks freely forward on the left side of the horse. The right arm is slightly bent, the left arm moves in a relaxed way.

If the horse has a tendency to not follow well, the leader walks in front of his head, a bit towards the side, lifts his right hand and attempts to lead it forward a bit without looking at the horse.
In case of spirited horses that rush forward, the leader stays back at the horse's shoulder and attempts to keep the horse next to him by applying gentle pulls to the reins. If the horse pushes forward energetically, the leader raises the left hand in front of the horse's face until it calms down.

If the horse kicks out at the leader with front and hind feet, he will stay close to the horse's shoulder and punish it by hitting the horse's chin with his right hand.

With double bridle

All four reins are placed on the horse's neck. The right hand reaches above the left curb rein, grasps the bridoon reins and parts them with the index and middle finger, one hand width underneath the rings. Otherwise, the procedure is the same as for snaffle bridle. [The curb reins are not held while leading.]

When the presenting recruit is abreast the superior, he stops, takes a small step forward with the right foot and turns right about face [180 degrees] on that foot in the direction of the horse, placing his left foot a step to the side. The right hand than grasps the left, the left hand the right snaffle rein, thumbs on the snaffle rings. If the horse is in a snaffle bridle, the rein ends are picked up.

One then softly pulls forward or exerts light pressure on one or both sides to position the horse in a way that will make him square up equally on all four legs. The horse's head is raised a bit.

In order to present the horse, the man now steps towards the horse's left side and stands there. If the horse is in a snaffle bridle, the reins are arranged in the same manner as for leading the horse and left long enough to not disturb the horse's gait. When leading the horse back, the recruit turns right about face with the horse [180 degree turn].

8. Mounting and Dismounting.

With snaffle bridle

For the purpose of mounting, the rider stands next to the horse and turns to the right [facing the horse]. The left hand grasps the reins, the right hand lets them go and reaches over the horse's neck to grasp the right rein, which is offered by the left hand. The left hand grasps the left rein between little finger and ring finger at a length reaching up to the withers, throws the end of the rein to the right side of the horse's neck and receives the right rein from the right hand and holds it in the full hand, so that it hangs down across the left rein on the left side.

Then the rider [facing the horse] steps towards the right and so far back as needed to be able to place the left foot into the stirrup. The left hand grasps the mane. Then he grasps the stirrup leather with the right hand, places the left foot into the stirrup up to the ball of the foot and then places the knee against the saddle, without having the tip of the foot touch the horse. He then rises up on the ball of the right foot, grasps the cantle with the right hand, holds on to the mane, puts weight onto the stirrup with his left foot, presses the left knee against the saddle and catapults himself up by pushing off energetically with the right foot, while tilting the upper body forward. Then he brings the right hand as a support for the upper body to the pommel, lifts the right leg high over the cantle and softly glides into the saddle. The right foot is placed into the stirrup and the reins are arranged.

When dismounting, the rider uses the left hand to throw the rein end that is hanging down on the left side to the right, places the right rein over the left, with the rein end on the left side. The rider then places the left hand on the mane and supports himself, while having the right hand on the pommel. He lets go of the right stirrup, puts weight into the left stirrup and raises the seat After bringing the right leg over the horse, the rider elastically descends onto the right foot, whereby the left knee remains firmly against the saddle. Then he takes the left foot out of the stirrup and places it beside the right foot. The rider then turns to the left, takes a step forward and once again arranges the reins to lead the horse.

With double bridle

The procedure for mounting is the same as with snaffle bridle with stirrups. After the step to the right side, the rider takes the reins with military rein hold [all reins in the left hand] so that he feels a little bit of tension. He then places the ends of the reins onto the right side of the neck.

When dismounting, the reins are arranged the same as during mounting, otherwise the process is the same as for snaffle bridle. Recruits [pupils] must also learn to mount without stirrups by jumping into the vault-on position, left hand on the crest, right hand on the pommel.

Part B. Riding Theory

II. Seat and Aids.

9. Rider's Seat and Posture.
(See figures 8-14, 18, 32, 37-45, 48, 51, 52, 54-61)

Bild 8.

Richtiger Sitz im Halten.

Figure 8: Correct seat in the halt

The two seat bones and the 'fork' [pubic arch] serve as the basis for the rider's seat. With relaxed muscles, the full breadth of the buttocks rest on the horse's back. The thighs rest against the saddle; their inner broad surfaces are turned far enough inward to position the knee flat against the saddle. One places the knees as far back as sitting on both seat bones will allow. This will enable a deeper position of the knee, which is especially important since it allows the rider to better envelop the horse with his legs and will bring the rider deeper into the saddle.

Figure 9:
Incorrect
Seat
(Collapsed
hip during
the turn)

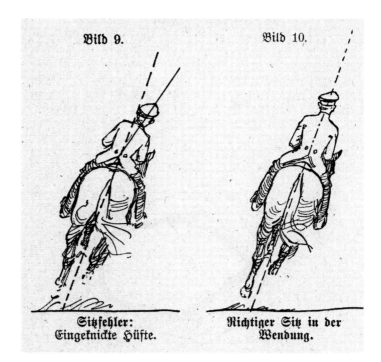

Bild 9.

Bild 10.

Sitzfehler:
Eingeknickte Hüfte.

Richtiger Sitz in der
Wendung.

Figure 10:
Correct Seat

If the thigh is rotated in a way that makes the knee cap point outwards, it results in a hollow or open knee, which does not allow a secure seat (see figure 12). By the same token, a thigh that is turned inward in an exaggerated fashion—knee stiffly pressed against the saddle—compromises the rider's suppleness, pushes the lower leg away from the horse's body and thus eliminates the rider's influence.

The upper body, mainly resting on the two seat bones, ascends vertically from the hips. The hips are positioned at equal height above the saddle and must not collapse to one side (see figure 9 and 10). The back is moderately braced. Hollowing of the back stiffens the seat (see figure 14). The shoulders must be dropped naturally and freely taken back so that the chest opens up. The head is carried freely and upright, without extending the chin forward; the gaze is directed over the horse's head. The upper arms are suspended from the shoulder joints without being pressed against the body (see figure 8). The inner surface of the forearm's middle part gently leans against the body. Pressing the elbows against the body will lead to pulled-up shoulders (see figure 11) and a stiff hand. Splaying the elbows out and away from the body negatively affects the seat and the rein position. The hands are lightly closed and carried vertically—thumbs up—so that the outside surface of the

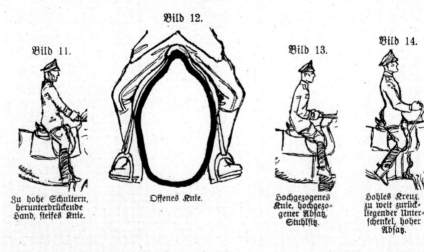

Sitzfehler:

Bild 12.

Bild 11.

Bild 13.

Bild 14.

Zu hohe Schultern, herunterdrückende Hand, steifes Knie.

Offenes Knie.

Hochgezogenes Knie, hochgezogener Absatz, Stuhlsitz.

Hohles Kreuz, zu weit zurückliegender Unterschenkel, hoher Absatz.

Examples of incorrect seat:

Figure 11:
Shoulders too high, hand pushing down, stiff knee

Figure 12:
Open knee

Figure 13:
Knee pulled up, heel pulled up, chair seat

Figure 14:
Hollow back, lower leg too far back, high heel

forearm in combination with the back of the hand form a straight line.

The manner of carrying the reins and holding the hands is described in more detail in subparagraph 13 "Rein Position and Rein Aids."

Depending on the length of the rider's legs, the lower legs hang down on the horse's body, more or less slanted backwards and maintain a soft contact with the flat calf. If a perpendicular line is drawn through the shoulder joint, it should end approximately at the heel. The tips of the feet are slightly pointing away from the horse. The heels are slightly pushed down. Attempting to force the tip of the foot to point in or out is equally wrong.

The stirrups must be adjusted to a length that allows the rider to maintain a deep knee and a low heel, while maintaining soft contact with the horse with his lower leg. If the stirrups are too short, the result is a pulled-up knee and buttocks that are pushed out too far back (chair seat). If the stirrups are too long, the rider is tempted to sit more on the 'fork' than on the buttocks ('fork seat'). Both scenarios are wrong since the rider is unable to give a driving leg aid. When riding cross-country or jumping, the stirrups are shortened a bit.

When jumping (figures 37-42) and riding cross-country (figures 45, 48, 51) and when working with horses with weak backs or weak hindquarters, one must minimize the load on the back and on the hindquarters. For this purpose, the rider leans slightly forward with his upper body. Thus he prevents his seat bones from exerting pressure onto the horse's back and transfers more of his weight onto his thighs and knees and therefore onto the horse's sides. If one wants to create additional freedom for the back while jumping and riding across uneven ground, the rider can slightly lift himself out of the saddle with his head raised, while noticeably pushing his hips forward. The lower legs must remain in their position. A tighter knee grip and slightly increased support by the stirrup will enable the rider to maintain a secure seat. The upper body must not be bent so far forward that the seat becomes insecure and the rider loses some control over the horse.

The most important aspect is the flexibility of hip and knees. The broad inner surface of the knee must never leave the saddle. Suppleness of shoulder, elbow and wrist joints ensure that the body's movement is not transferred to the hand and the horse's mouth is not disturbed.

10. Aids. General Remarks.

The rider influences the horse with weight, legs, and reins. By nature, the leg aids are driving aids, the hand aids are restraining aids. Both are effectively supported by the rider's weight influence.

The driving aids are much more significant than the restraining aids.

11. Weight Aids.

The art of moving with the horse depends on the ability to harmonize one's own center of gravity with the horse's center of gravity during all movement as it changes position.

If the rider transfers his weight to the left or right side, the

34

horse receives the impulse to deviate from the current line into this direction. This weight aid is executed by putting more weight on the respective seat bone. When doing so, this hip will be slightly lowered and the knee moves into a deeper position. Collapsing in the hip is a mistake that results in a weight transfer to the wrong side.

12. Leg Aids.

The leg is responsible for influencing the hind foot on the same side. The closer it is positioned near the girth, the more the hind foot will be encouraged to step forward (**forward driving leg**); when the leg is positioned further back, it will either stop the hind foot from leaving the track (**guarding leg**) or prompt it to leave the track (**sideways driving leg**)—depending on how strong the leg aid is applied.

For a horse that is well gymnasticized and goes on the bit in good self-carriage and with impulsion, soft contact with the lower leg will suffice to keep it in form, gait, and pace, provided that the seat is correct. The pressure and activity of the leg, however, must be increased in relation to the degree of movement desired by the hind feet or the desired degree of control over them.

During movement, the leg only correctly influences the hind foot on the same side to step forward at that moment when the hind foot pushes off the ground.

In case the leg aid does not suffice, it is amplified by the spur, first with light pressure, then with stronger pressure. Most of the time skilled contact will suffice. The leg position must not be changed during the process.

For ticklish mares or mares in heat, one avoids the spur aids and uses a riding cane to reinforce the driving aid. The spur wheels must be dulled in order to exclude the possibility of injury during use.

13. Rein Position and Rein Aids.

a) Rein position (figures 15-18)
With snaffle bridle
The snaffle reins are grasped between the little finger and the ring finger without twisting the rein and held at equal length, so that the smooth

Figure 15:
Hand position with snaffle bridle

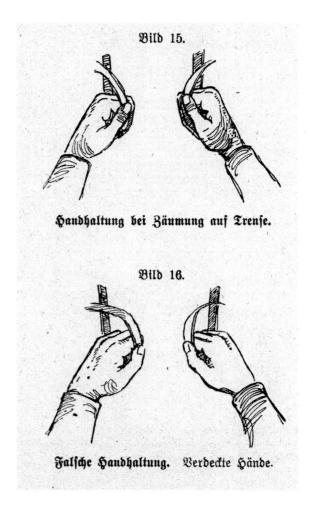

Bilb 15.

Handhaltung bei Zäumung auf Trenſe.

Bilb 16.

Figure 16:
Incorrect hand position
Covered hands

Falſche Handhaltung. Verbedte Hände.

surface of the leather faces outward. The ends of the reins hang down on both sides on the outside of the reins over the second joint of the index fingers. The hands are closed, the thumbs are slightly curved and press the reins onto the second joint of the index fingers. The hands are carried vertically, thumbs up, the reins enveloping the horse's neck, at about four finger widths apart, at such a height that allows the forearms and the reins to form one continuous, straight line [from bit to elbow].

For double bridle

The rider separates the two curb reins with the ring finger of the left hand, while the ends of these reins hang from the hand down to the right across the second joint of the index finger.

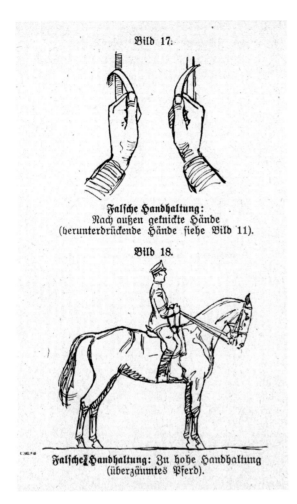

Bild 17.

Falſche Handhaltung:
Nach außen geknickte Hände
(herunterdrückende Hände ſiehe Bild 11).

Bild 18.

Falſche Handhaltung: Zu hohe Handhaltung
(überzäumtes Pferd).

Figure 17:
Incorrect hand position: Hands bent outwards (for hands pushing down see illustration 11)

Figure 18:
Incorrect hand position: hands too high (horse overbent [behind the vertical])

The right hand takes the snaffle rein with the thumb and the first three fingers and draws it through the left hand until the left snaffle rein and the left curb rein have an equal amount of tension. The right snaffle rein is held short enough to be of equal length with the right curb rein. The remaining portion of the snaffle rein is dropped towards the rider's body, towards the inside and down.

When riding with "3 and 1" rein hold, the left hand remains positioned vertically above the withers and in front of the center of the body, holding the snaffle rein. The right hand is also carried vertically at a distance of about two fingers breadth from the left and at the same height.

When riding with "2 and 2" rein hold, the rider holds one curb rein and one snaffle rein in each hand, while the reins in the left hand are parted by the little finger, the reins in the right hand are parted by the ring finger.

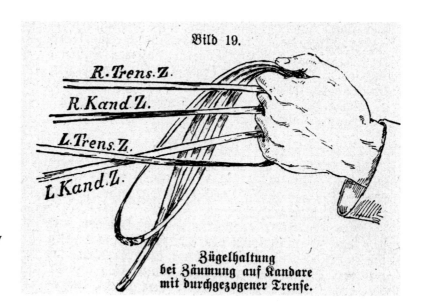

Figure 19: Military rein hold

R. Trens. Z.

R. Kand. Z.

L. Trens. Z.

L. Kand. Z.

Zügelhaltung
bei Zäumung auf Kandare
mit durchgezogener Trense.

[When (asked or) commanded to ride with military rein hold (4 reins in one hand)], the curb reins and the left snaffle rein are held in the same fashion as a 'held snaffle' [3:1 rein hold]; the right snaffle rein is grasped between the middle and index fingers, all four reins are placed over the second joint of the index finger and held here by the left thumb (figure 19).

The rider's right arm hangs naturally from the shoulder, the hand rests lightly, open and relaxed behind the thigh, its inner surface pointing towards the horse's body.

The normal manner of holding the reins during work is with 'held snaffle' [3:1 position]. When riding cross-country, the rider can separate the reins [holding one snaffle and one curb rein in each hand, 2 and 2].

During jumping and climbing the reins must be separated. When riding with a weapon in the right hand, the rider uses 'military rein hold.' Riding with 'drawn-through' snaffle [military rein hold, riding with all reins in the left hand] must be practiced frequently: this has the advantage of getting the rider used to a lighter contact and makes him independent of the reins and enables him to use weapons [with the right hand]. It also serves to test the horse's self-carriage, even when rein contact is light. The rider must be capable of riding longer distances, while holding the reins in one hand.

38

a) Rein Aids

The hand influences transmitted to the horse via reins and bit are called rein aids. They are created by means of increasing or releasing tension on the reins. Since by nature the rein aids have a primarily restraining effect, they must always be combined with driving aids.

The more responsive the horse is to letting the influences of the hand come through the jaw, the poll, the neck and back into the hind end, the better and faster these aids work. Only when the horse is completely responsive to the finest aids ["through-ness"], will it be fully obedient to the hand.

A horse that willingly yields to the hand influences by bending the poll and neck gives the rider the feeling of a secure and soft connection between hand and horse mouth in the halt as well as in motion. This is called "the horse goes on the bit." A horse that looks for support in the reins and presses down on the rider's hand "leans on the bit;" a horse that cancels out the connection between hand and horse's mouth by evasively moving the head back is "behind the bit." A horse that reacts to a yielding hand by attempting to evade the bit by pushing forward-up with poll and neck muscles, goes "against the bit" [also "above the bit"].

The art of good rein position is based on the ability to continuously maintain the connection between the rider's hand and the horse's mouth. This is called "contact" (also see subparagraph 62).

The yielding rein aid means that the little finger of the stationary hand is allowed to move closer to the horse's mouth or—without losing contact—the hand temporarily moves forward as much as the situation requires. If a yielding rein aid is meant to allow the horse to lengthen the neck, it is necessary to move the entire arm forward, to let the horse stretch on the rein and consequently let the reins slide through the fingers. In this case the rider therefore lets the horse 'chew' the reins out of his hands.

The non-yielding rein aid is used for horses that take too much contact as well as during all half-halts (subparagraph 27). During the non-yielding rein aid, the rider leaves the hands in place, closes them tightly and bears the increased pressure, until the horse once again pushes off the bit and becomes light. Precondition for this non-yielding rein aid is the rider's elastically braced back, while buttocks are pushed forward. It is of utmost importance that the rider's hand becomes light at the same moment when the horse becomes light on the bit.

The asking rein aid is used when the non-yielding rein aid is not sufficient during half-halts and for the purpose of turning. It is executed by closing the hands more firmly and turning them inwards; in the process, the middle finger joints move closer to the rider's body, the little fingers rise up. If a stronger influence is needed, the arm must participate in the asking aid. The warning not to get stuck in retraction especially applies to the asking rein aids. These aids must never degenerate into pulling. Instead, they must be refreshed in a lively alternation with yielding aids, in case the aids are not immediately successful.

The horse will react to a one-sided pull on the rein by bending the head and neck to the respective side and turning around. In order to properly execute a turn and limit the bend of head and neck, it is necessary to counteract with the outside rein. This aid is called a **"guarding rein aid."** This aid consists of a slight resistance applied by the hand but can be increased to an asking rein aid.

Most riders have the incorrect tendency to influence the horse too much by the use of the hands and too little by means of leg and weight aids. This tendency must be continuously discouraged.

For rein aids during turns see "Turns during Motion," subparagraph 21.

When riding with a double bridle with 3-to-1 rein hold, turns are usually executed in the same manner as they are when riding with a snaffle bridle.

In order to check whether the horse has self-carriage during freer gaits as well as a calming aid, one "gives and retakes" the reins. Here the rein hand touches and slowly moves up and down the crest, without attempting to maintain contact with the horse's mouth; in the process, one must not abandon the driving aid.

III. Putting the Horse on the Bit and Yielding of the Poll.

14. Putting the Horse on the Bit.

Putting the horse on the bit means to push the horse from back to front in such a manner that a completely secure but light contact is maintained between the rider's hand and the horse's mouth, during the halt as well as during motion.

During the halt, the rider braces his back and uses his legs to push the horse forward against the lightly supporting hand, until it steps under with its hind legs and chews on the bit.

The legs rest against the horse's body, guarding and ready to encourage a hind foot to step forward in case it breaks out sideways or to the rear, by tapping, rather than squeezing, with the leg on the same side. If the horse steps forward with a front foot, the rider tightens the rein on the same side until the horse places the respective foot back to the correct position. If the horse places the front feet underneath its body, the rider encourages the horse to place them forward by using squeezing leg aids at the girth. As soon as the horse stands still in the desired position and starts chewing on the bit, the rider discontinues the resistance with the hands and lets them rest quietly in their position.

A horse that is correctly put on the bit gives the rider the feeling of a soft seat, equally loading all four feet.

During motion the rider uses the above described aids as soon as he feels that the horse is no longer chewing on the bit, loses energetic forward movement and no longer has sufficient contact.

15. Yielding of the Poll.

For the purpose of yielding of the poll the rider repeats the aids described in 'putting the horse on the bit' until the horse volunteers the neck and poll bend that is needed for the effectiveness of the reins and is appropriate for its conformation. If a horse stiffens neck and poll against the rider hand, driving aids must be used to encourage the horse to push off the bit. For horses whose education is considered completed, the quickest way to reach this goal is often a skilled application of the spur.

41

Sitting heavily into the saddle, however, must be avoided on horses with a soft back and weak hindquarters. Most of the time it is advisable to start by performing turns on the forehand from the halt and thus encourage the horse to push off the bit and only then get the horse to first yield at a shorter pace, then as soon as possible at a fresh working trot on a circle. If a horse is insubordinate, forward movement is always the rider's best ally. For full control of an evasive hind foot, it is recommended to temporarily increase the distance between the hands. Some riders attempt to force a bend in the poll by pressing down the hands and stiffening hands and arms (see figure 11), often combined with raising the buttocks. This must be strongly discouraged. **A bend in neck and poll must only be the result of driving aids against the supporting hand.**

If the horse lowers the head slightly too much, meaning it leans on the bit in a low position and is looking for support in the rider's hand or if it evades the influence by curling up the neck, the rider must energetically ride the horse forward in animated steps without rushing. In the process, the hands are moved to a lower position, initially move forward, then support, while the rider uses legs and back to ride the horse forward. This encourages the horse to carry the head higher and put the nose in front of the vertical or to lengthen the curled-up neck. This elevation unloads the horse's forehand, distributes more weight to the hindquarters and therefore ensures the leverage effect of head and neck on the back and hindquarters. The resulting improved balanced self-carriage of the horse enables freer and more energetic gaits.

IV. Development of the Gaits.

16. Move-off into the Walk.
(See figures 52, 56, 60)

During the transition from the halt to the walk, the rider pushes the horse—which is put on the bit—with his back and both legs into the forward movement while simultaneously giving a yielding rein aid. One must never strive for contact at the expense of a ground-covering, steady, fluid walk. Horses that jog must be put onto the bit by means of driving aids and then transitioned down to the walk by applying half-halts, but should not be held back by the hands.

17. Move-off into the Trot, Transitions within the Trot.
(See figures 54, 55, 58, 59)

The aids for move-off into the trot mirror those for move-off into the walk. For the well-ridden horse, the only thing the rider needs to do during the trot is ensure that the horse maintains the speed with impulsion and rhythm and softly goes on the bit with the neck in proper position, while chewing on the bit.

In order to increase the speed, the legs drive the horse forward more assertively. The transition must be fluid, the aids must not be pouncing. The hand lets out the more extended steps without abandoning the connection with the horse's mouth. The freer the speed, the more the rider is required to go with the movement, otherwise he stays behind the movement. If a horse reacts to the aids by falling into the canter, it must first be brought onto the bit in the canter by means of driving aids and must only then be transitioned down into the trot by application of half-halts.

18. Rising Trot.
(See figures 54, 55)

The rising trot significantly lessens the impact of the rider's weight on the horse's back and joints. It makes it easier for the horse to breathe and push off and step under with the hind legs. It also tires the rider less than the sitting trot.

The rider does not sit every one of the horse's steps, but—supporting himself with knees and stirrups—absorbs one step in this position and sits softly into the saddle after the following step, buttocks pushed forward. The upper body rises during the forward movement of a diagonal foot pair, meaning the right hind foot and the left front foot or vice versa, and lowers when the same leg pair makes contact with the ground. The rider therefore returns to the saddle each time when either the right or the left hind foot makes contact with the ground. Therefore one accordingly says that the rider posts the trot on either the right or left hind foot. The rider can tell which hind foot is swinging forward by looking at the simultaneous forward movement of the opposite shoulder. When riding in the arena, one always trots on the inside hind foot because only if the inside hind foot is encouraged by the inside leg aid to step forward far enough can it properly support the rider's body weight during turns and in the corners. When changing the rein [direction], the rider must change the hind foot on which he posts by sitting the trot one or an uneven number of steps and then rising again when the new inside hind foot steps forward.

The rider will notice an equally comfortable feeling during the trot on the left and on the right hind foot as proof for the fact that the horse has been schooled equally on both sides. During the rising trot, the rider must not let the horse fall apart. Instead, he must always maintain a light but determined contact with the bit. For this purpose, he must also be able to drive during the rising trot. This is accomplished by keeping his upper body straight, pushing hips and buttocks forward every time he sits into the saddle and continuously maintaining contact with the horse's body with the lower legs, while absorbing the movement with supple knees.

The horse's gait and softness can only be facilitated during the rising trot if one strives to encourage the hind feet to step far forward. The horse's self-carriage will be impaired when the rider falls forward during the rising trot, pushes the buttocks backwards with a soft back, lets the reins slack and splays out the legs with stiff knee and ankle joints. **The rider must be thoroughly educated and trained in the rising trot**; the driving effect of the rider's weight—weighing on the saddle during the sitting trot—can only be replaced by lively activity of the lower legs and by good posture of the upper body.

Therefore one should also place special emphasis on the rising trot during inspections. During longer rides one must change the hind foot in order to ensure that one of the diagonal foot pairs will not be strained more than the other (see subparagraph 60).

19. Move-off into the Canter, Transitions within the Canter, Transition to the Trot, Counter Canter, Change of Lead in Canter
(See figures 57, 61)

The rider gives the following aids to **move off into the canter**:
The inside leg at the girth encourages the hind foot on the same side to step forward. This changes the current foot fall and the horse is prompted to transition into the canter. At the same time, the outside leg remains on the horse's body in a guarding position; a half-halt with

44

the outside rein limits the extent to which the outside hind foot steps forward. The rider's weight rests predominantly on the inside seat bone.

When transitioning into the canter, one must be vigilant to ensure that the horse is not put on two tracks.

As soon as the horse rises, the rider must release the canter movement with a lightly yielding hand and apply driving aids to get the strides going. The upper body must follow the horse's movement well; the rider's inside seat bone is pushed forward and he takes his outside shoulder well forward.

If a horse transitions into the canter on the wrong lead, the rider must transition the horse down, straighten it and only then transition into the canter again in the correct position. When riding in a detachment [in the arena], horse and rider must leave the track for this purpose.

In order to shorten the canter strides, the rider must gradually restrain the strides rather than suddenly hold the horse back. For this purpose, more weight must be transferred to the hindquarters. This is done by using the leg aids to encourage the hindquarters to increasingly step under, while using half-halts, especially on the outside rein. Half-halts and yielding are performed in the rhythm of the strides. Once the horse has gained self-carriage, the hands become more passive. The leg aids should encourage the hindquarters to perform even and lively strides. Even in a shortened working canter, the energetic springing action of the hind legs should be noticeably felt under the rider's buttocks.

A canter extension must occur softly and fluidly; the driving aids must not start suddenly. The faster the speed, the more the rider's seat must follow the movement. Moreover, the rider must continuously strive to maintain the horse's 'through-ness' by means of half-halts, in spite of a stronger contact with the bit.

In order to be able to securely and fluently transition into the trot, the rider must have his horse firmly on the bit during and after the halt and straighten it again, push it into the trot with both legs and follow the horse's movement with his upper body, while maintaining an elastically braced back. A fidgety seat, a hard hand, as well as any one-sided or pouncing leg influence often causes the horse to start cantering again. In order to prevent this mistake it is advisable to place the horse into a slight shoulder-in position during the downward transition and maintain this position during the first steps of the trot.

Before counter cantering, the horse must be put into the respective position. It is only ridden in a shortened working canter and only practiced while riding independently in a group, not when riding in a detachment. In order to change the lead, the rider carries out a transition into the walk, sits and changes flexion, then develops a new canter. This is executed only by individual riders, upon the command "Change canter lead," and not when riding in a detachment (or group.)

V. Exercises on a Level Track [Flat Work].

20. Turns on the Spot.

Turns on the spot can be executed on the forehand or on the haunches. When turning on the forehand, the pivot point is always the horse's inside fore foot; when turning on the haunches, always the horse's inside hind foot.

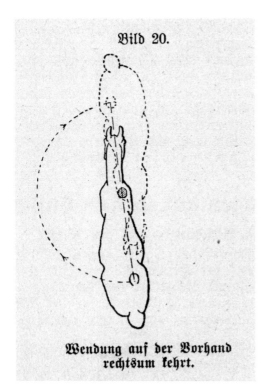

Bild 20.

Wendung auf der Vorhand
rechtsum kehrt.

Figure 20: Turn on the forehand to the right.

By alternately performing multiple partial turns on the haunches and the forehand, the horse can be moved sideways on the base line. For this purpose, the rider usually begins with a turn on the haunches, followed by a turn on the forehand, etc.

a) Turns on the forehand

The turn on the forehand serves to teach rider and horse the effect of the one-sided [uni-lateral] aids. The rider first puts the horse on the bit and flexes the head slightly towards the direction of the turn. The inside leg behind the girth then presses—aided by the inside

46

rein, if necessary—the haunches step by step around the forehand until the turn is completed. In the process, the inside hind foot steps across and in front of the outside hind foot. The outside leg is behind the girth in a guarding position and firmly counteracts every other step made by the hind foot, so that there is a pause between every step. This prevents the haunches from rushing around. During and after the turn legs and back ensure that the horse remains on the bit and does not hide behind the bit. Stepping forward will usually cause the horse to fall out through the outside shoulder. This must be prevented by counteracting with the outside rein. Stepping back is less of a mistake. Turning on the forehand cannot be practiced on the outside track next to the kicking board since there is not enough room for the horse's neck and head.

b)   Turn on the haunches
       For the turn on the haunches, the rider first puts the horse on the bit and flexes it towards the side of the turn. The inside rein initiates the turn. The pivot point is under the inside hind foot. The rider uses both hands to guide the forehand, step by step, around the haunches in an arc. For this purpose, he brings his outside shoulder forward, uses his outside leg to prevent the horse from falling out through the outside hind foot and uses his inside leg to encourage the inside hind foot to lightly step forward under the weight. Stepping forward is less of a mistake than stepping back.
       If the turn is performed next to the kick board of the arena, the horse will have moved away about one horse's width

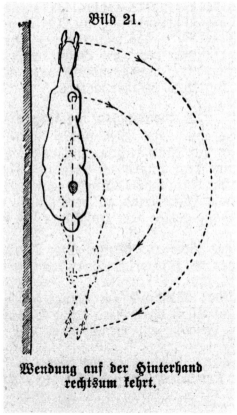

Bilb 21.

Wendung auf der Hinterhand rechtsum kehrt.

Figure 21: Turn on the haunches to the right.

from the kick board during the turn. After completion of the turn, the horse must be brought back to the track in a forward-sideward movement.

21. Turns during Movement.

The rider can only execute precise and tight turns during movement if he is able to give the horse an even longitudinal bend, which corresponds with the curve of the turn and thus can prompt the haunches to follow exactly the track of the forehand.

During a correct turn, the horse is required to increasingly support the body weight with the inside hind leg.

Before each turn during movement, the rider collects the horse with a half-halt and shifts his weight slightly towards the side of the turn.

The horse is flexed towards the side of the turn. The inside rein leads the horse into the turn, the inside leg at the girth drives the hind foot on that side forward. The outside rein controls the head and neck position by providing some resistance, guards the outside shoulder, determines the degree of the turn and—together with the guarding outside leg—prevents the horse's outside hind foot from falling out. The better the rider succeeds in prompting the inside hind foot to provide proper support and the outside hind foot to step forward into the direction between the front feet during the turn, the tighter and faster he can turn his horse.

All turns require proper weight distribution. Only if the rider pushes his inside hip forward while his knee remains deep and lets his outside shoulder follow the forward movement, will he be able to properly guide the horse's forehand and prevent the horse's haunches from falling out.

Once a turn is completed, the horse is straightened. If the riders were riding with position before the turn, each rider now resumes this respective position on the new rein without being commanded to do so.

22. Riding through Corners.

In order to ride through corners with precision, the rider applies a half-halt—mainly with the outside rein—three steps before the corner, meaning before the turn begins. At the same time, he gives the horse position and turns with the inside rein on the arc of a volte through the corner. Depending on the horse's level of schooling, gait, and speed as well as the rider's skill, the arc may be ridden flatter accordingly. In all other regards, the execution is the same as for the turn during movement.

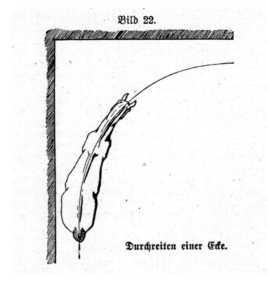

Bild 22.

Durchreiten einer Ecke.

Figure 22: Riding through the corner

In order to evade the tighter bend, horses try to flatten the arc through the corner or to place the inside hind foot sideways. This must be counteracted by the inside leg and the outside rein. It is wrong, however, to attempt to force the horse to move deeply into the corner by applying outward pressure with the inside rein, since this causes the horse to fall through the outside shoulder.

If there is no kick board, the horses often try to evade the stronger bend by bending to the outside before reaching the corner. The outside guarding aids must keep the horse on the track to prevent this. The aids described above must be applied accordingly during turns and change of rein on the long diagonal.

23. Riding on a Circle.

Riding on a circle compels the horse to increasingly support the body weight with the inside hind leg and to bend it more than it does on a straight line. It therefore prepares the horse for turns and for the canter.

In order to ride the circle exactly, the horse must be continuously turned and longitudinally bent in accordance with the arc of the circle. Here, it is especially important to fix the neck at the shoulders. In the walk and in the trot, the horse's inside hind foot steps into the track of the front foot of the same side—if the horse is bent correctly; the outside hind foot must follow the track of the outside front foot.

When transitioning into the circle, the rider shifts his weight slightly to the inside. The rider's inside leg—close to the girth—drives the hind foot on the same side forward, the inside rein turns onto the circle line at the halt point. The outside leg—behind the girth—prevents the haunches from falling out. The outside rein supports the outside leg aid and keeps the neck aligned at the withers.

Repeated changes of rein from circle to circle and through the circle is a good method to bring the horses to suppleness and onto the aids.

Tightening the circle: While shifting his weight more to the inside, the rider turns the horse with the inside rein, supported by the outside leg, from the outside sideways-forward towards the center of the circle. [When riding in a group...] the individual riders thus reach the smaller circle on a gradually tightening circle line by simultaneously moving forehand and haunches towards the inside.

When **enlarging the circle**, the outside rein and the inside leg gradually expand the arc of the tightened circle.

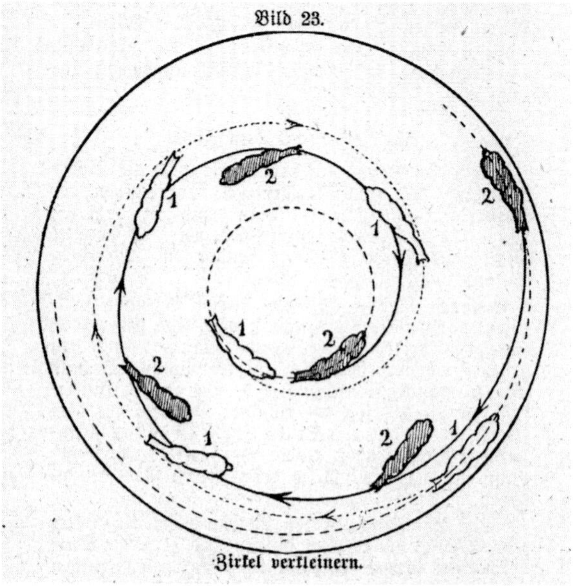

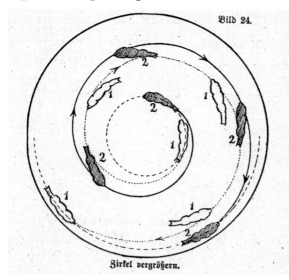

Figure 23: Tightening the circle.

Figure 24: Enlarging the circle.

50

24. Volte, Half Circle and Back to the Track and Figure Eight.

A volte of 6 meters in diameter represents the maximum of longitudinal bend that a horse can produce without adversely affecting the gait. Voltes and half circles of 6 m diameter are only ridden in the walk or in shortened working gaits. In the beginning, the schooling level of the horse must be taken into consideration by expanding the track. In this case they can be ridden in a **working gait**; this also applies to the figure eight. The aids are the same as for turns and riding on a circle.

25. Serpentines.

Serpentines serve the rider as a good method to teach the horse obedience to the turning aids. When riding serpentines, the rider must rely mainly on weight aids to initiate a change of direction in the horse (see Figure 1). Apart from that, the aids are the same as for turns in motion. Serpentines are only ridden in the **walk, the working and the shortened working trot.**

26. Half Pirouettes in the Walk.

The half pirouette in the walk is a turn on the haunches during motion. It is only executed in the walk. The rider first applies an energetic half-halt with the outside rein and then applies the aids for turning on the haunches. The half-halt, however, must not result in a complete stop. The interruption of the forward movement must be immediately followed by guiding the horse into the turn.

27. Half-halts and Halts.

a) Half-halts
They serve to transition the horse into a shorter gait, to improve rhythm and self-carriage of the horse during a gait, to regain lost self-carriage, and to respond to a horse that presses on the bit or rushes during the gait.

During a half-halt, the rider tightens the reins as if intending to stop the horse, while continuing the driving aids. Often, a non-yielding rein aid while simultaneously bracing the back is sufficient.

b) Full halts

Full halts bring the horse to a stop by application of asking rein aids. They are—especially in stronger gaits—prepared by applying half-halts. The asking rein aids—in an energetic sequence of asking, yielding and repeated asking—must be repeated until the horse stands. Each rein aid is accompanied by driving aids and thus the horse is pushed up from back to front. Horses with a weak back require a light seat with a well-braced back during the full halt. As soon as the horse stands still and shows the desire to lengthen the neck, the rider must cease the asking rein aid and become light in the hand.

If the rider is in a position to decide at which distance he would like to stop his horse, the rider must consider the strength and speed of gait and the through-ness of the horse. The stronger and faster the gait, or the less 'through' the horse is, the sooner the movement must taper off.

28. Rein-back.

The rein-back is a method of increasing through-ness and obedience.

For the rein-back, the rider puts the horse on the bit and uses alternating rein pulls—which directly affect the hind feet—to prompt the horse to step back with one diagonal leg pair after another, with even and calm steps in a straight direction. In the process, the legs only rest in a guarding position on the horse's body in order to prevent the horse from letting his haunches fall out or evade and from freeing himself from the rein.

Any increase to the load on the horse's back makes it increasingly difficult for the horse to lift and set back the hind legs; the rider must therefore not sit too deeply when the horse refuses the rein-back, but instead slightly lean forward with his upper body.

The turn on the forehand is a proven method to motivate a horse, who plants his hind legs out, to step back. The rider gives the rein-back aids when one of the hind feet steps under the body.

29. Straightening.

The influences used by the rider to align the forehand with the haunches are called **straightening**. The straightened horse—moving on one track—should always align the longitudinal axis of its body with the track, irrespective of whether the track is straight or curved. Only then, the driving power of the hindquarters acts in a straight direction and fully affects the forehand.

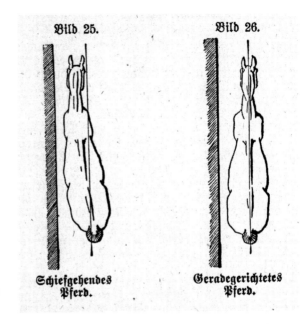

Bild 25.

Bild 26.

Schiefgehendes Pferd.

Geradegerichtetes Pferd.

Figure 25 : Crooked horse.

Figure 26: Straightened horse.

The fulfillment of this requirement is made difficult by the peculiar tendency of most horses to carry themselves crookedly. As a result of this crookedness, front and hind feet do not track up. The fact that the horse is narrower in the forehand than in the hindquarters further contributes to this crookedness.

With rare exceptions, it is usually the right hind foot that the horse finds harder to place straight forward under the body. In case of crookedness, e.g. towards the right, the rider uses the right rein to guide the right fore foot in front of the right hind foot and drives the horse with a dominant right leg aid towards the right rein. Straightening work must be executed while riding energetically forward.

30. Bending.

Bending serves the purpose to increase the horse's obedience to the sideways rein pulls and to get the outside of the horse's neck to stretch. This exercise helps the rider to achieve through-ness, giving to the inside aids and reaching for the outside aids, as well as an

53

improvement of self-carriage and gait.

Bending is of little value if neck and head are worked too much while standing versus working the whole horse in motion, mostly in the trot.

Bending while standing only serves the special instruction of rider and horse. For this purpose, the horse must be on the bit and carry the nose somewhat in front of the vertical. The rider turns the bending hand as if to turn and causes the horse to turn his head towards this side while keeping his ears on the same horizontal level. The outside hand yields at first, then applies a supporting rein aid to prevent too much yielding to the inside rein and keeps the neck straight at the withers. The crest must always tip towards the inside. The muscles on this side become flat and bulge out on the outside.

If the horse tilts in the poll—which can be observed as one ear standing lower than the other—the rider must elevate the horse's lower ear by temporarily lifting the respective rein hand.

Bending is most effective in the working trot, later in the medium trot.

The rein aids for **bending in motion** are the same as for bending while standing. The inside leg must encourage the inside hind foot to energetically step forward and—together with the shortened inside rein—must demand flexibility of the inner side. As soon as the horse yields to the inside rein, the outside rein comes into effect. Outside leg and rein guard the haunches and shoulder, and together ensure that the entire horse bends evenly around the inside leg. The neck should not be bent laterally any further than the horse is able to bend in the lumbar vertebrae.

Bending should not be started before the horse has gained an even contact with the reins, has fixed the neck on the withers and yields in the poll according to its schooling level. When bending at the halt, it is imperative to ensure that all four feet stand still; during motion the gait must remain rhythmic.

31. Leg-yielding.

Leg-yielding teaches the rider how to use the one-sided leg and rein aids and teaches the horse obedience to these aids.

The head is always flexed towards the leg that drives the horse sideways, which thus becomes the inside leg. On the arena's rectangle, the rider may let the horse yield on the long sides to the left as well as the right leg; on the circle, he must only let the horse yield on the leg facing the center of the circle. During leg-yielding, the lateral flexion of the neck must be limited to a minimum. Bending the neck beyond this minimum will cause the horse to fall over the outside shoulder and weaken the horse's neck musculature.

Leg-yielding is only practiced in the walk and working trot and only over short distances. One must not ride through corners while leg-yielding. When leg-yielding, the horse moves on two tracks, which are up to one step apart, while maintaining a slight head flexion; the inside feet step forward evenly and across the outside feet.

The rider sits more towards the inside and presses the haunches sideways with the inside leg, which is positioned right behind the girth. This pressure must occur when the inside hind foot lifts off the ground and is, if necessary, repeated with every step. The outside rein continues to guide the forehand on its track. The rider must counteract the horse's attempts to escape the leg and to fall over the outside shoulder by guarding with the outside rein and leg.

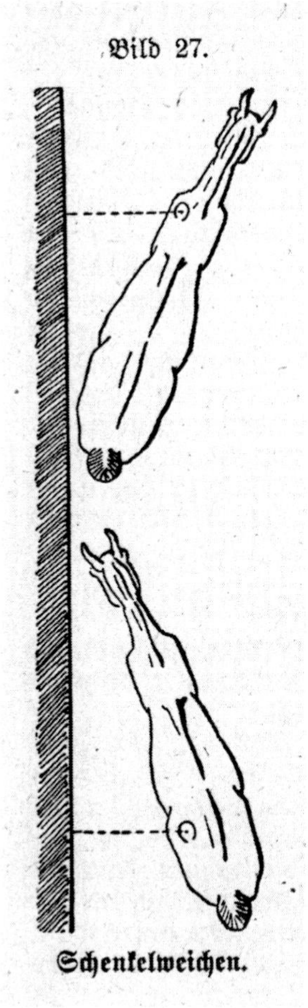

Bild 27.

Schenkelweichen.

Figure 27: Leg-yielding

If the horse is to yield to the leg that faces the inside of the arena, the rider guides the forehand a small step towards the inside of the rectangle or circle, as if starting a volte; the haunches remain on the original track. The rider then applies a half-halt and begins the leg-yielding.

Leg-yielding is concluded by aligning the forehand with the haunches.

If the rider wants to let the horse yield to the leg facing the outside of the rectangle, he applies a half-halt as soon as he has ridden through the first corner of a long side, far enough to let the horse's head reach the next side. He then assumes the respective position that lets the horse yield to the leg. To conclude leg-yielding, the rider changes the horse's flexion, leads the horse back to the track on a flat arc and continues to ride straight ahead.

Yielding to the leg outside of the rectangle only serves the initial education of rider and horse during the beginning of schooling; yielding to the leg that faces the inside of the arena is of higher value for schooling, especially since it prepares for the shoulder-in.

32. Tightening and Enlarging the Rectangle.

In order to solidify the obedience to the sideways driving leg aid and the guiding outside rein, the exercise "tightening and enlarging the rectangle" is ridden.

During the exercise "tightening and enlarging the rectangle"—just like during leg-yielding—the horse moves with minimal head flexion on two tracks, which are up to one step apart. The better the horse is on the outside aids, the smaller the

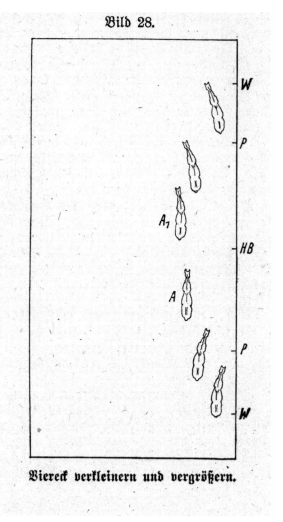

Bilb 28.

Biered verkleinern und vergrößern.

Figure 28: Tightening and enlarging the rectangle

56

angle [of the horse relative to the track] and the more this exercise evolves from a suppling exercise to a collecting exercise. The exercise is ridden at the walk or at the working trot. If the horse's schooling is advanced, it can also be executed in a shortened working trot.

The extent to which the horse is led into the arena when tightening the rectangle depends on its level of schooling (same applies to enlarging the rectangle, accordingly). At first, one must only demand little.

After riding through the corner, the rider gives the horse the respective flexion, lets the horse push off the previously outside, now inside rein and pushes it—sitting more towards the inside—with the now new inside leg forward-sideways towards the inside of the arena, starting no sooner than at the marker [W]. The previously inside, now outside leg maintains the forward movement.

At A (see figure 28), the rider aligns the forehand with the hindquarters by means of a turn on the haunches during movement, rides at least one horse length straight ahead, sits and changes the flexion, and at A 1 presses the horse with the new inside leg back to the large track until the Marker [W] is reached. There, the horse is first straightened, then correctly ridden through the corner.

33. Riding 'in Position' and 'outside Position.'

The horse moves 'in position'[3] when the active influence of the outside aids maintains a uniform longitudinal bend . In this bend, the inside hind foot tracks into the direction of the inside front foot, the outside hind foot tracks in the direction between the front feet. The crest of the horse's mane is tilted toward the inside, the rider sees a glint of the horse's inside eye and inside nostril.[4]

---

3   *in Stellung*

4   ["In riding 'in position' (also known as the 'second position') the horse moves with its inside forefoot and [inside] hind foot on the same track. The outside foot follows a track slightly (at most half a hoof-width) inside that of the outside forefoot, so that from the front the outside hind foot is visible between the forefeet...

" Note: Whilst in the shoulder-fore it is principally the inside hind leg which is made to step closer to the outside one, in riding 'in position' it is the outside hind leg which 'narrows the track' by stepping closer to the inside one.

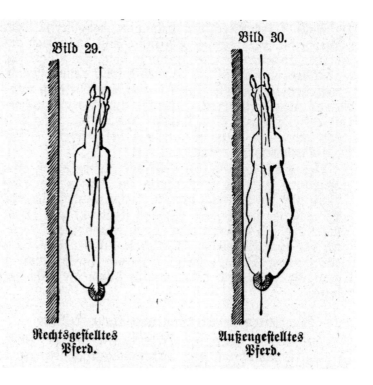

Figure 29: Horse positioned to the inside [right]

Figure 30: Horse positioned to the outside [left]

Bild 29.

Bild 30.

Rechtsgestelltes Pferd.

Außengestelltes Pferd.

For riding through corners, for turns, school figures, for shoulder-in and the shortened working canter, the above described or a lesser degree of bend is required. [During group instruction] each rider must independently position his horse during these exercises without being ordered to do so.

While riding in 'position to the outside' [or 'outside position'], the horse is positioned to the outside of the arena and must therefore turn against his bend. Seat and aids are the same as for riding 'in position,' except when riding through corners and other turns. During a turn, the outside feet [outside of the bend] move on a smaller circle [they are toward the inside of the arena] than the inside feet. Therefore the rider

---

"AIDS: The aids for riding 'in position' are only slightly different from those to the shoulder-fore. Special care should be taken that:

"The rider's inside leg maintains the activity of the horse's inside hind leg and keeps it on the inside track;

"The rider's outside leg keeps the horse's outside hind foot tracking in between the prints of the forefeet." From *Advanced Techniques of Dressage German national Equestrian Federation*, Translated by Christina Belton, Kenilworth Press, 2000, Page 49-This passage added for clarity.—*Editor's note*]

58

must limit the forward movement of the outside feet with the leading outside rein.[5]

[When riding in position to the outside in turns and circles,] in order not to impede the evenness of the gait, the inside hind foot [closer to the outside of the arena]—which carries more weight—must be prompted to step forward further. This is done by reducing the bend.

If 'positioning' and 'positioning to the outside' is to be ridden as a special exercise, it is always necessary to give the respective command. As such, it must only be ridden in the walk and the shortened working trot. In order to achieve uniform softness on both sides, the position must be changed often accordingly. The change of position must occur fluidly, so that the horse can transition from one position to the other without pausing or rushing.

The most common and gravest mistake when riding in position is to demand the head flexion by holding the inside rein too tight or by pulling on it and thus making it impossible for the horse to correctly step forward and under with the inside hind foot.

34. Shoulder-in.
(See figure 59.)

The shoulder-in can be ridden when the horses have gained through-ness and self-carriage in the shortened working trot and are able to move in position. This exercise especially facilitates straightening.

Shoulder-in is ridden in the **walk and the shortened working trot**. Ideally, the development of this movement begins after riding through the first corner of the long side.

During shoulder-in, the horse is slightly flexed to the inside, goes in well-collected self-carriage and thus with the respective elevation of the forehand. Its forehand is angled towards the inside of the arena up to one step away from the track of the outside hind foot.

To develop the shoulder-in, the rider shortens the inside rein, flexes the horse to the inside, applies a half-halt and turns the horse towards the inside without increase of neck bend, as if executing a volte. By applying a second half-halt with the outside rein, he prevents the

---

5   [The inside is always the side to which the horse is flexed or bent.—*Editor's note.*]

horse from further moving towards the
inside and continues to guide the horse in
the lateral movement.

Bild 31.

During the lateral movement, the
inside rein provides the head position,
ensures that two tracks are maintained
and—together with the inside leg—
prevents the hindquarters from falling in.

The outside rein in conjunction
with the outside leg regulates the bend
and elevation and guides the horse.

The inside leg, closely behind the
girth, is tasked with maintaining the bend
of rib cage and encouraging the inside
hind foot to energetically step forward;
only secondarily it acts in conjunction
with the outside rein to prompt the lateral
movement of the horse.

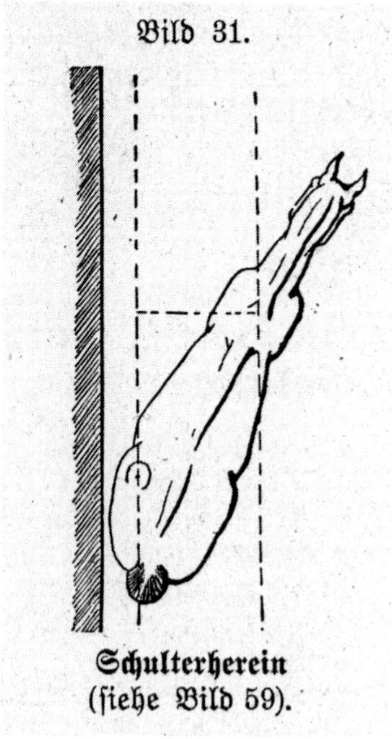

Schulterherein
(siehe Bild 59).

The outside leg guards the
hindquarters and encourages the outside
hind foot to step forward. The position of

Figure 31: Shoulder-In.
(See figure 59).

the outside leg depends on whether it is guarding or driving.

The rider must not make the mistake to come behind the
horse's movement but must always follow the movement properly. The
shoulder-in must stop two horse lengths before the first corner of the
short side. Corners and the short side are ridden in good collection and
with position on one track. The shoulder-in is concluded by aligning the
forehand with the hindquarters.

It is of special value to the education of rider and horse to
execute a transition from shoulder-in to a volte on one track. After
concluding the volte, one can either ride straight on or again transition
into the shoulder-in.

Another useful exercise is the full halt in the shoulder-in; here
the outside aids must act predominantly. The most common mistake
when practicing shoulder-in is that the horse falls through the outside
shoulder. Excessive use of the inside rein—and therefore excessive
neck bend—contribute to this. The rider must eliminate this mistake by
resisting with the outside rein and energetically driving the outside hind

Bodenrickarbeit.

Figure 32: Cavaletti work

foot with the outside leg.

Horses that—in spite of driving aids—stay behind the bit during the shoulder-in must first be ridden onto the bit by riding in a freer gait on single track.

VI. Training over Cavaletti, Jumping, and Cross-country Riding.

35. General Remarks.

Exercises over cavaletti, across obstacles and in open terrain are just as necessary for the thorough schooling of rider and horse as exercises on an even track [flat work]. They are a good means to familiarize rider and horse with one another and to produce suppleness.

They are so very beneficial for the education because, during the execution of these exercises, it is harder for the rider to align his center of gravity with the horse's center of gravity, and because they pose different and diversified challenges to the horse, they are of great educational and gymnastic value.

During this type of schooling one must pay special attention to appropriate preparation and well-thought-out progression of challenges, and ensure that—in case difficulties arise—limits are set at the right time. Excessive demands in the beginning lead to tensions in rider and horse.

A. Cavaletti Work.

36. Purpose and Execution.

Cavaletti work serves the schooling of the young horse (subparagraph 66) as well as the schooling of young riders on older horses (subparagraph 87). This work is executed in the walk and the trot.

Cavaletti are wooden, movable obstacles, which are about 1.5 m wide, up to 20 cm above the ground and must not be too light.

The preparation work starts with the horses stepping over individual poles at the walk. This is followed by riding over individual, low cavaletti in the same gait and in the trot. When this is securely mastered, the horses are ridden over several (first two to three) cavaletti, placed one behind the other, in the trot. This method teaches the horse to step in rhythm, to work in his joints and teaches the rider a feeling for a **horse's swinging back**.

The requirement of **4 cavaletti at a distance of 1.4 m** must not be exceeded. Initially, this exercise must not be repeated too often and not at an overly fast pace. Excessive sudden demands can lead to overstrain and damage of the joints, especially in young horses.

Positioning the cavaletti on the track makes the work easier. In order to save time, it is recommended to mark the proper distance measurements on the kicking board.

B. Jumping.

37. Preparatory Jumping Exercises and Jumping in Hand.

Before one approaches jumping training under the rider, which exceeds the limits of training planned for young horses, the horse must be prepared by extensive suppling exercises, including cavaletti work

62

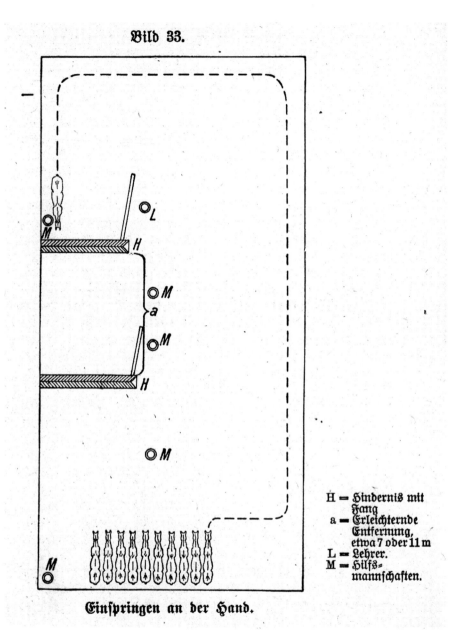

Einspringen an der Hand.

Figure 33: Jumping in hand

H = Obstacles with wing
A = Facilitating distance of around 7m or 11m
L = Instructor
M = Helpers

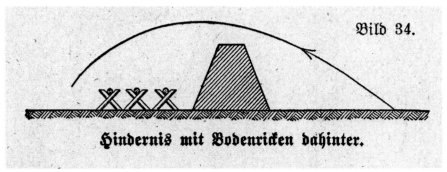

Figure 34: Obstacle with cavaletti behind

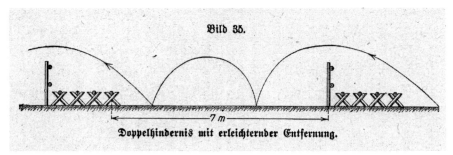

Figure 35: Double obstacle with simplifying distance

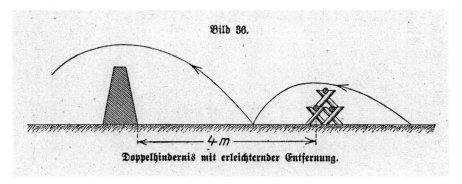

Figure 36: Double obstacle with simplifying distance

and by preparatory jumping exercises. Outdoors, one can also ask for an extended canter. The horse can also be prepared by loose jumping.

The purpose of **preparatory exercises under the rider** is to have the horse tackle many low obstacles and thus teach him obedience, activity of the back, confidence and agility, and to teach the rider a feeling for the aids, flexibility of the seat, and security.

For this purpose, one moves off in the walk or in the trot. If the horse starts to canter before the obstacle, the rider calmly sits the canter. After tackling the obstacle, he continues to ride in the original gait in which he moved off.

Jumping in hand in the arena as preparation for greater demands is also done with horses that have already been suppled by other exercises.

For this purpose, the detachment dismounts and stands on the far side of the jump at the short wall, facing inward, stirrups fastened. The side of the detachment that faces the long wall towards the obstacle will remain at a distance of four steps from the long wall. The reins are pulled through the throat latch and knotted on the neck. Starting with the side of the attachment that is further way from the obstacle, the horses are individually led to the obstacle. The rider hereby walks on the outside. In order to catch the horses, one places a helper with a grain bucket on the other side of the obstacle. The instructor—holding a whip—stands before the obstacle, but should only make use of the whip if the horses hesitate to jump.

Once the horses are familiar with the process, one can add obstacles on the opposite long side. One or two people suffice to block the corners. The side of the obstacles facing the inside of the arena is conveniently delimited by use of wings that are taller than the obstacle.

Loose jumping is intended to teach the horse to collect itself, to pace the canter strides before each jump and to jump with a supple back. This [supple back] can be identified by the fact that the neck-back line from the poll to the tail forms an upward arched arc. (Figures 39 and 40)

Horses that find it difficult to develop the proper movement sequence are improved by training over obstacles that are wider in diameter, especially at the take-off and landing point. For this purpose, one uses cavaletti that are placed so closely together that the horse is unable to step in between and must jump them as if it were the surface of a trench.

In detail, the following rules apply:

Mistakes	Arrangement of obstacles
Horse does not arch the neck-back line upwards during the jump, meaning has a tense back	Place one or several cavaletti closely together behind the upright obstacle. The horse will not see them until he is in the air. This will prompt it to "dive" with neck and head (See Figure 34.)
Horse takes off too late and does not stretch	Spread obstacles and long jumps, using cavaletti placed closely together before the obstacle (See Figure 35.)
Horse jumps too flat	A number of upright obstacles at distances of approx. 3 to 3.5 or 6 to 6.5 m (so called handicap).
The horse takes off too soon.	One or several cavaletti close behind an upright obstacle (See figure 34.)
Horse does not pace the last canter strides before the obstacle well	Low obstacle (50 cm) at a distance of approx. 4, 7, or 11 m in front of an upright obstacle (so-called simplifying [opposite of handicap], see figures 35 and 36.)

During loose jumping work over several obstacles placed one after another, there is a risk that horses easily unlearn how to let themselves 'fly.' In between exercises they must therefore repeatedly be schooled at a lively pace over a single obstacle, placed in the middle of the long side.

38. Rider during the Jump.
(Seat during the jump see subparagraph 9 and figures 37 – 42)

One moves off towards the middle of the obstacle at a right angle. If the horse looks at the obstacle it must be given as much freedom of the rein as it asks for, without giving up contact with the horse's mouth or ceasing the driving aids. For horses that jump insecurely, the driving aids increase up to the moment right before take-off.

During take-off and suspension phase, the buttocks are slightly lifted out of the saddle, relative to the degree to which the upper body leans forward. Any kind of exaggeration in this posture makes the rider's posture insecure and decreases his control over the horse.

The upper body must follow the horse's movement during the entire jump. The rider's head must be held high, the gaze must be directed beyond the obstacle or trace the path which the rider intends to follow after having cleared the obstacle.

Knees and lower thighs rest snugly against the horse's body. The heels are pushed down; the feet may be placed into the stirrup up to the instep.

The horse stretches the neck during the jump. Therefore one must allow the neck the necessary freedom while maintaining a light contact. The rider must be flexible and yield in the elbow and shoulder joint.

It is wrong to try to indicate to the horse when to take off or to lose contact entirely. If contact ceases abruptly, the horse is disturbed.

During the landing the rider's knees serve as shock absorbers by elastically catching his entire weight. This unloads the horse's front legs.

If the horse stumbles during the landing, the rider lets the reins slide through his fingers so that the horse is entirely free to get up. A long rein enables the horse to better step under with the hindquarters and cannot pull the rider onto the shoulders of a horse that might be in the process of falling. The rider must increase his knee grip.

If—during a broad jump—the rider feels that the horse does not properly land on its hindquarters, he must shift the weight of his upper body more towards the front.

The hands are positioned low; during the jump, the right hand remains on the right, the left hand on the left side, below the crest. The rider yields [the reins] along the neck in the direction of the horse's mouth.

When yielding while holding the reins with one hand, the small finger of the closed rein hand slides along the crest.

As soon as the horse starts to display incorrect movements or habits at any particular moment while jumping over obstacles, these must be eliminated by arranging one or several obstacles in a special way. The respective instructions given for jumping in hand also apply to jumping

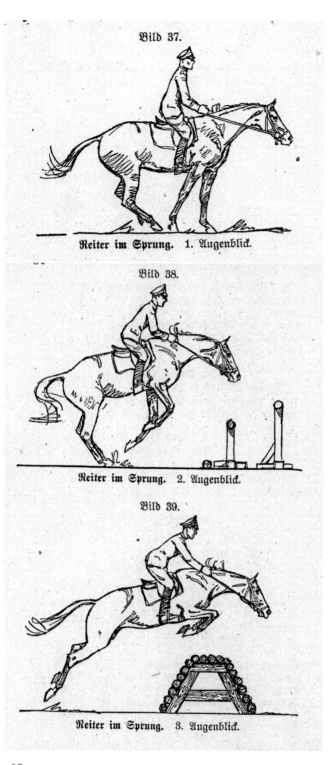

Bild 37.

Reiter im Sprung. 1. Augenblick.

Figure 37:
Rider during the jump - Phase 1

Bild 38.

Reiter im Sprung. 2. Augenblick.

Figure 38:
Rider during the jump - Phase 2

Bild 39.

Reiter im Sprung. 3. Augenblick.

Figure 39:
Rider during the jump - Phase 3

Figure 40:
Rider during the
jump - Phase 4

Bild 40.

Reiter im Sprung. 4. Augenblick.

Figure 41:
Rider during the
jump - Phase 5

Bild 41.

Reiter im Sprung. 5. Augenblick.

Figure 42:
Rider during the
jump - Phase 6

Bild 42.

Reiter im Sprung. 6. Augenblick.

under the rider, accordingly (subparagraph 37). When riding with a double bridle, the reins must be held in the 2:2 position, with dominant snaffle reins. If riding while holding a weapon, one must use military rein hold (see subparagraph 13 a, last section).

Incorrect seat during the jump

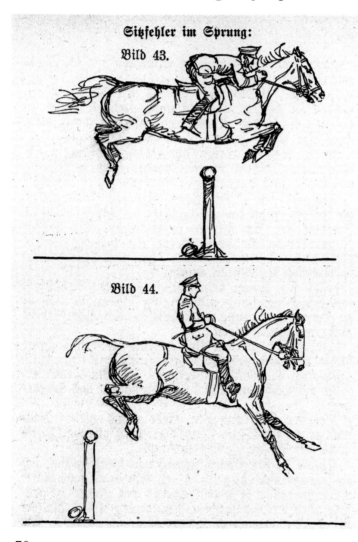

Figure 43: Buttocks too high, knee sliding backwards, heel slips up, rigid elbow joint (horse: topline broken down instead of arched upward)

Figure 44: Rider behind the movement, rigid shoulder and elbow joint (as a result, horse cannot stretch neck forward/down). Knee not lying flat against the saddle.

39. Conduct When Jumping Disobedient Horses.

Proper education of rider and horse, correct instruction, and a gradual increase of demands will prevent contumacies or limit them to exceptional cases. If they do occur anyway, the riding instructor must check whether the horse was not yet developed enough. In this case the dimensions must be decreased or one must use securely jumping horses as lead horses.

The riding instructor must always strive to reach the goal without application of punishment; only for extraordinarily dissobedient or stubborn horses is punishment an appropriate option.

If the rider does not yet have sufficient skill, he must be replaced by a better rider. A horse must never move on to the next level before at least eliminating the possible disobedience by means of a similar, but smaller obstacle. One must strive to get a disobedient horse to jump the respective obstacle under the weaker rider, too, who initially did not succeed in controlling the horse.

A riding crop may only be used by advanced riders. It must be held tip down in a supporting fashion on that shoulder side towards which the horse wants to break out. For the purpose of driving the horse forward, the riding crop is held in the full hand, tip up and used right before take-off. The crop must touch the horse closely behind the rider's lower leg. In order to avoid injuries to the horse's underside, one must only use inflexible short crops of about 1 m length.

a) Breaking out and jumping crooked

Most horses break out towards the left side because a turn to the left is easier for them (stiff right hind foot) and the rider is usually a bit more awkward and harder with the left hand than with the right hand.

In the following, the side towards which the horse intends to break out is called the "outside" and the other side the "inside."

When a horse shows the intent to break out, one must immediately completely relax the outside rein. Even the slightest contact is a mistake. The opposite hand keeps the contact or transitions to the asking rein aid. The driving aids continue. One proceeds in the same fashion with horses that jump crookedly, but here it suffices to relax the rein on the side towards which the horse pushes.

If a horse runs past an obstacle, it is immediately brought to a full halt. Then it is turned on the forehand towards the inside and the direction of the first approach and only then ridden to the middle of the obstacle to repeat the jump; the turn on the forehand can be repeated to gain obedience to the inside rein. When approaching the jump for the second time, there must be contact on the inside rein. The outside rein is relaxed.

b) Stopping and Rearing

If a horse stops immediately before the obstacle, it must be reined back at a right angle to the obstacle and then energetically be ridden towards the obstacle again until it clears the jump.

Horses that stop at some distance before the jump must be encouraged to move their hind feet by quickly repeating energetic driving aids. (Rearing horses see subparagraph 44.)

c) Rushing

If half-halts are unsuccessful, the goal should be reached by repeatedly jumping over low obstacles on a circle or in irregular sequence. At first, such horses must repeatedly be turned away at some distance before the obstacle.

d) Lazy and stoic horses

They must be encouraged to jump fluidly by applying energetic driving aids (legs, spurs or riding crop). Work in a pack can also be beneficial for them (see subparagraph 43).

C. Cross-country Riding.

40. Purpose of Cross-country Exercises.

The combination of exercises on a level track [flat work] and jumping with cross-country achieves optimum suppleness of rider and horse. For this purpose, it is necessary that during cross-country riding lessons the horses are also worked in an instructional manner. Time and again, the final aim—as described in subparagraph 62—must be ensured during cross-country instruction, even for old horses.

For this purpose one rides on large circles and long lines while keeping increased distances [to the next horse], only in the walk and working trot—generally posting the trot—or in the working or extended canter. One must only ask a working posture of the horse. The stirrups must be adjusted a bit shorter than in the arena.

While requirements for collecting exercises are lower than in the arena, one must slowly increase those requirements that pertain to agility and willingness of the horse in practical use exercises. This especially includes:

Frequent transitions into the canter left and right from the trot, frequent transition from the working canter to the extended canter and vice versa, full halts, standing calmly, rein-back.

41. Exercises over Uneven Terrain.

The first goal that needs to be achieved is the rider's ability to softly move with the horse's movement and thus take the load off the horse's back and not hinder the correct back activity of the horse. This unloading is achieved by cushioning the upper body with elastic hip and knee joints as well as shifting the weight onto both sides of the horse by shifting it onto the thighs. Shoulder and elbow joint must yield into the direction of the horse's mouth, which reaches forward-downward when

Bild 45.

Arbeit über Wall.

Figure 45: Schooling across a bank

going over uneven ground or obstacles. On occasion, the rider must lift the buttocks out of the saddle a bit. The leg must have a driving effect through pressure from top to bottom into the direction of the stirrup. The stirrup is imagined to be hanging freely when riding uphill or downhill. The foot may be pushed into the stirrup, the heel is low, the knee adheres so tightly to the saddle that it never slides to the front, nor to the back or up. The back is braced elastically, the shoulder is low, the head positioned freely towards the front.

Climbing exercises—initially over low trenches and banks— are especially beneficial. During this exercise the horses must round their backs and relax. Therefore this type of work is also a good means to supple horses under young riders, whose active influence is still imperfect. The lines of movement of rider and horse during up and downhill climbs are so similar to the ascending and descending part of a jump that climbing is also a very good preliminary exercise for jumping (figure 45).

42. Cross-country Jumping.

Cross-country jumping training is especially significant since it is much easier to create inviting obstacles in the country. Obstacles in the

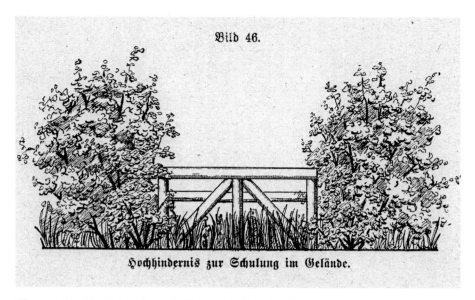

Bild 46.

Hochhindernis zur Schulung im Gelände.

Figure 46: Upright obstacle for schooling in the country

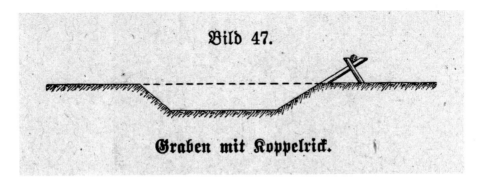

Bild 47.

Graben mit Koppelrick.

Figure 47: Trench with wooden pasture fence

country must have the following advantages compared to obstacles in the arena:

They can be built completely solid. Solid obstacles are more educational for the horse than movable obstacles.

They must be integrated into the terrain. The young rider and the young horse will learn to jump easier if the risk of breaking out is minimized. Therefore obstacles for learning riders and horses must be bordered on the sides by natural boundaries and are therefore best constructed in ravines, on forest aisles, or between bushes.

Such bordered obstacles can be narrow. Narrow obstacles have the advantage that the horse is unable to flutter [sway to left and right] in front of them. This minimizes the risk of the horses developing the habit of jumping crookedly (see figure 46).

Obstacles are appropriately created to match the terrain's natural vegetation around the obstacles foot print. This makes the take-off easier. Bare wooden pasture fences are one of the most difficult obstacles and therefore not suitable for riding students.

Schooling over trenches is better done in the country than across artificially created trenches, which always have a defect of some sort or another.

Wider trenches are easier to jump if there is a low pasture fence or a so called 'brush' in front of them (see figure 47).

Flexibility of both rider and horse are further much improved by jumping up and down and by jumping on a hill. For all unfamiliar obstacles one must initially use secure lead horses. Before increasing the dimensions of obstacles, clearing an obstacle must be a non-issue for rider and horse.

Bild 48.

Auffprung eines in der Ausbildung
fortgeschrittenen Pferdes.

Figure 48: A horse with advanced schooling jumps up.

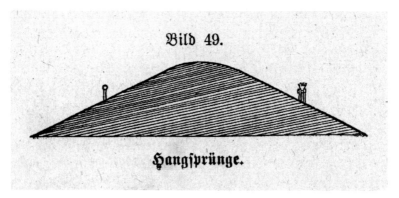

Bild 49.

Hangsprünge.

Figure 49: Hill jumps

43. Schooling in a Group.
Individual Cross-country Riding. Hunting.

A special form of cross-country instruction is **schooling in a group**. Its purpose is to take advantage of the herd instinct and the forward drive of the horse in order to overcome fear. This type of work is especially suited to encourage horses to let themselves fly over broad jumps. On the other hand, schooling in a pack has the disadvantage of reinforcing the horse's herd instinct.

Every time one schools in a pack, it is therefore necessary to incorporate **individual riding**. The riding instructor must be careful to present only tasks that are—according to the previously observed condition of the horse—likely to result in obedience. This especially applies to young riders and horses. For this purpose one asks the horses— first in pairs, later individually—to perform transitions to a slower pace and lower gait, while the pack departs at faster pace or in a higher gait in straight direction. This alternation between schooling in a pack and individual riding is especially essential for fierce horses.

Only when this training without obstacles has been completed, can horses effectively participate in hunts. For hunts obstacles must either have a natural border on each side which prevents breaking out, or must be long enough for the field to clear them comfortably side by side. The art of creating hunts lies in fitting the obstacles to the terrain and in increasing demands slowly and unnoticeably.

A hunt participant must observe the following rules of conduct:

Gazing far ahead, he chooses his path and rides an even pace. He avoids crossing other horses or pushing against them, especially in front of obstacles. (Therefore the need for long obstacles!)—He does pass other horses from behind while riding at fast pace. This spoils the horses since they are not trained to canter calmly.—He never rides too closely behind the rider in front of him, since this would endanger him, in case he falls.—He will ride a fierce or insecurely jumping horse on the outer wings. If he loses control over the horse, he leaves the hunt field, riding in a large arc out of the field.—If a horse becomes disobedient, it must never block the path of other riders. The horse can be ridden towards the obstacle again later.—If the horse falls, the rider tries to separate himself from the horse by moving to the side and rolls over the shoulder without letting go of the rein. This way he is considerate of the hunt field which is thus not endangered by his abandoned horse and preserves himself the opportunity to continue his ride.

If done correctly, hunting is of high educational value for the rider.

VII. Conduct on Disobedient Horses.

44. Correct Education

Correct education will turn obedience into a habit for the horse so that serious contumacies[6] will be the exception. Disobedience will most frequently occur in badly ridden and incorrectly schooled horses.

When disobedience occurs, the rider must not merely have in mind to enforce his own will, but instead also strive to recognize and remedy the causes for the disobedience.

It is easiest to overcome disobedience on supple horses. On tense horses, however, the chance of successful application of aids is much lower, and the possibility that unsuccessful battles with the horse will result in further disadvantages for his education is much greater.

The fastest and most secure way to correct disobedient horses is by having a good rider work with them. For unskilled riders, who are unable to effectively apply their aids, the disobedience can quickly grow into fierce contumacy.

When correcting disobedient horses one should always part the reins.

If circumstances dictate that obedience must be forced by a fight, the rider must maintain his calm and deliberateness in spite of the needful energy. If punishment does become necessary, however, it must be applied with vigor.

Pointers for the correction of the most common vices are provided below. The suggestions for riding instructors apply especially to groups of young riders and young horses.

---

6   Acts of stubborn perverseness or rebelliousness; acts of willful and obstinate resistance or disobedience to authority.

a) Shying horses

Riding Instructor	Rider
The horse is ridden past the object, in the pack behind lead horses. The pack is slowly disbursed, eventually the lead horses are taken away.	The rider initially does not flex the horse's head towards the scary object, but rather towards the side towards which the horse wants to evade and drives it past the object with the head turned away, meaning if the object is on the left side, he leg yields to the right.

b) Horses that buck and rear after mounting

Riding Instructor	Rider
The horse must be relaxed by working without a rider, meaning work on the lunge, jumping in hand or running freely in an arena before mounting. The horse must be saddled for some time before mounting. The girth must only be tightened after the saddle has been on the horse for some time.	The rider tries to ride the horse forward. If this fails, the rider sits lightly and cushions the blows with an elastic knee/ankle joint while his upper body leans forward. During rearing the rider also bends the horse towards the more supple side—if needed, all the way to his knee.

c) Horses that stick to other horses or to places

Riding Instructor	Rider
First the horse is ridden out of the loose detachment with two neighboring horses serving as lead horses. Slowly the lead horses move away, the distances are slowly increased. Initially, one can hold a feed bucket in front of the horse or lead him by the cheek piece. The same procedure can be applied when sticking to places.	The rider puts the horse calmly and increasingly on the bit, flexes it—if it pushes against the neighbor horse—to that side and increasingly applies the inside leg. If needed, he takes the horse a few steps back. Then he drives with energetic driving aids, if needed supported by clucking.

d)   Bolting horses

Riding Instructor	Rider
Since the cause for this vice is most often that horses have not been familiarized with running in a pack in faster gaits with frequent downward transitions to the walk, this exercise must be repeated frequently.	The rider, with elastically braced back, applies one-sided, decisive rein pulls and then yields again. He tries to turn the horse away in a large circle and then tighten the circle.

VIII. Schooling the Horse without a Rider.

45. Equipment for Schooling on the Lunge Line.

One requires a lunge line of about 7 m length, a whip that is long enough to touch the horse at any time with the lash, and a pair of side reins. Lunge cavesson and surcingle come in handy.

One can use reins that each are twice as long as the distance from the saddle to the mouth to put the horse in side reins.

On each side, the reins are fastened to the attachment strap, then laced through the snaffle rings and then attached to the girth at a height that depends on the respective purpose. Instead, one can also use regular side reins. The reins must have the same length and must be adjusted so that there is only very light tension on the reins when the horse is in a relaxed posture. One must never restrict the horse's neck under any circumstances.

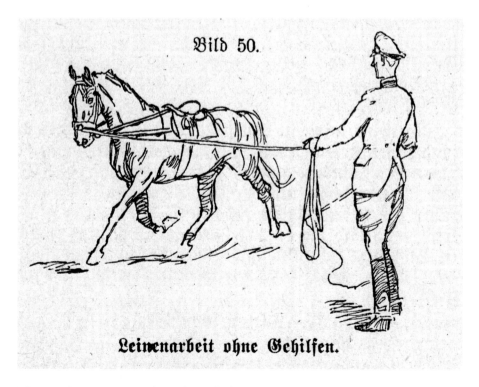

Bild 50.

Leinenarbeit ohne Gehilfen.

Figure 50: Lunge work without helper

46. Conduct of the Lunger and his Helper.

When working on the lunge line, the person who lunges chooses his position in a way that will continuously keep him slightly in front of the horse's head.

Lungers who want to school their young horses on the lunge line must involve a helper, who is charged with leading the horse and handling the whip. Lunger and helper must work in exact accord with one another. They always approach the horse slowly from the front.

The lunge line is then fastened to the ring of the lunge cavesson or into the bridle's chin strap, having the pin of the buckle point towards the horse's chest. The inside hand (on the left rein therefore the left hand) holds the lunge line at the same height as the horse's mouth, while the outside hand holds the loop and the folds of the rest of the lunge line. (Manner of holding the lunge line without helper, see figure 50.)

47. The Lunge Aids.

The lunge aids are only effective if the horse has contact with the lunge line, meaning "is on the lunge."

These aids are moving the horse out of the circle, bringing the horse into the circle, and halts. Bringing the horse into the circle is used when horses pull out of the circle. One repeatedly tightens the lunge line, which must each time immediately be followed by yielding. When moving horses that push into the circle out of the circle, one wiggles the lunge line towards the horse and points the whip at the shoulder at the same time. Halts and half-halts are applied by repeatedly putting more tension on the lunge line, then yielding the lunge line or by lightly shaking it.

48. The Whip Aids.

The whip aids serve to drive the horse forward. The whip is always held in the outside hand. To start, it is pointed at the horse's croup, whereby the arm is stretched out from the shoulder. The whip lash drags on the ground. Once the horse is schooled in the work on the lunge line, one lowers the arm until the tip of the whip is at the same height as the hocks.

If it becomes necessary to drive more, one moves the whip lash from the back to the front and from bottom to top in circular movements or one touches the horse with the tip right above the hock.

49. The Voice Aids.

The voice is an essential aid. Whip and lunge aids should always be prepared by the voice. One must always use the same commands. For the purpose of calming the horse or shortening the gait, one gives the command in a drawling tone; for driving and lively work, in a short tone.

If the voice is continuously utilized in the correct manner, the horses will assume the desired gait without hesitation upon vocal command.

50. Schooling of the Horse on the Lunge Line.

One begins with the left rein, since the left turn is easier for the horse.

The helper, staying behind the lunge line, leads the horse on the inside rein on the track for some time at the walk, so that it can get to know the arc of the circle and learn to stay on it.

Upon the lunger's command, the horse then transitions into the trot, while the helper pats its neck and speaks to it in a calming voice. He continues to hold the rein in the trot. After some time, one transitions down to the walk. These walk and trot exercises are repeated several times. If the horse stays calm, the helper lets go of the rein and walks with the horse, staying closely behind the lunge line and a few steps away from the horse. As soon as he notices that the horse intends to rush forward, he grabs the lunge line and, if needed, once again the snaffle rein.

This way one prevents the horse—in many cases—from bolting away at a canter, which is inconvenient and can be dangerous for the young horse.

Once the horse has calmed down, the helper slowly walks along the lunge line in the direction of the lunger and steps behind him.

If—in spite of all precautions—the horse bolts forward, one should let it canter if the canter is not too fast. At the same time, one speaks to it with a calming voice and—after some time—calms it down by giving the command 'trot' and shaking the lunge line.

Should this attempt be unsuccessful or if the canter so wild that the horse is at risk of falling, the helper approaches the horse from the front with his arms raised, in order to catch the horse, calm it down, and lead it off again.

If there is no border around the circle and the horse breaks out of the circle line, the lunger resists the horse. While resisting, it can be necessary to slowly let the horse pull the remaining folds of the lunge line out of one's hand in order to minimize bruising. Once again, the helper leads off the horse.

For lively horses, it is advisable not to use the whip during these initial exercises. The voice—in combination with raising the outside arm—often suffices as a driving aid.

Only when the horse has calmed down does the helper pick up the whip very carefully.

Once the horse just about maintains a circle line at a calm trot, one transitions down to the walk, then to the halt. The horse must be praised for its obedience.

For the purpose of changing the rein, which will only be done once the horse has fully calmed down, one starts by leading the horse around. One can later have the horse carry out a turn on the forehand while touching it with the whip.

The schooling lesson is concluded by having the horse walk without side reins for a longer period of time. It is especially important to consider the physical strength and condition of the young horse during the initial exercises.

After some time, once the horse has lost its fear of the new work, it will willingly move forward in its natural posture. Now it is important that the horse learns to trot evenly and calmly. In the process, it must reach for the reins and lunge line.

Side reins for horses that carry their nose too high are adjusted lower; for those that carry their nose too low, higher.

For young horses, one must adhere to the principle that they should reach for the reins, but must not be put on the rein.

Common consequences of side reins that are adjusted too

tightly are: unnaturally narrow necks with pushed-down lower neck line [ewe neck], lack of suppleness, especially in the back, loss of free shoulder movement, or tense, unclean gaits with lack of impulsion.

If the horse lowers the neck and searches for the rein, it must be able to find it.

One must always bear this principle in mind while schooling the horse on the lunge line. The length of the side reins needs to continuously be corrected during the work on the lunge line.

The pace of the work must be a fresh working trot, which can be extended a bit from time to time.

If one wants to develop the canter, this is best done from a calm trot, whereby one disturbs the trot movement by lifting and pulling the lunge line, gives the command to 'canter' several times in succession, and drives with the whip.

If the horse does not jump into the canter and instead rushes forward in the trot, one needs to slow the speed down and start over.

The goal is to achieve a natural canter and to keep the canter exercises initially brief. If the horse does not stay in the canter and reverts into the trot in spite of the driving aids, this is usually a sign that the horse finds it hard to maintain the canter. In this case, one stops the exercise, lets the horse rest and then asks the horse to canter once again. After the canter, one lets the horse trot a bit and then walk.

The goal of lunge work is achieved when the young horses, with necks stretched forward, nose pointing forward/down, with contact on the rein and on the lunge, trot, canter, and walk completely calmly and with complete suppleness.

51. Chewing the Bit and Flexing in Hand.

Letting the horse chew the bit in hand is a means to teach the horse to yield in the poll and in the jaw as a response to the bit's pressure on the bars. It has the advantage that it can be performed before the horse has learned to carry the rider's weight and before knowing how to listen to leg aids.

The rider stands in front of the horse and grabs the right snaffle rein with the left hand, and the left snaffle rein with the right hand, right below the snaffle rings. Both rein ends are in the left hand. The rider then starts to put pressure on the horse's bars with the snaffle bit—starting softly, then alternating sides with even pressure—in order to encourage the horse to yield in the poll. As soon as it shows that it is inclined to do so, the rider yields, so that the horse's mouth starts chewing due to the increased softness.

Once the horse has gotten used to the pressure of the bit on both bars, one starts flexing the horse in hand.

The rider stands in front of the horse and grabs the reins in the same way as for 'chewing the bit.' If he wants to flex the horse to the right, for example, the left hand takes the horse's head and neck to the right side—now the inside—while the right hand pulls the rein forward and towards the right side of the flexing horse. Depending on the situation, the right hand pulls into a higher or lower direction.

The rider must harmoniously coordinate the effect of both hands in that the horse's neck and must only participate in the flexion to an extent in which the crest tilts to the inside and the flexion happens predominantly in the throat latch [head/neck junction].

52. Lateral Movements in Hand.

This exercise improves suppleness and obedience to unilateral aids.

One begins on the left rein. The horse is put on one outside fixed snaffle or side rein in such fashion that head and neck are positioned straight ahead. The rider stands in front of the horse's inside shoulder, grabs the inside snaffle rein right below the snaffle ring and uses the riding crop (about 120 cm long and elastic), which he holds in the right hand, to drive the horse's hindquarters around the forehand by touching the horse right above the hock. During this exercise, it is more important to have the horse step forward/sideways, rather than just having it step over sideways. If the horse holds back and does not want to move forward, it must be repeatedly pulled forward with the hand. If needed, one supports this movement by driving forward with the crop. The hand that holds the reins must by no means pull backward. Initially, one should be satisfied if the horse walks around as if walking a normal volte with its forehand. This way the horse eventually learns to turn on the forehand as schooling progresses.

IX. Working with Horses with Conformational Flaws.

53. For Horses with Conformational Flaws

It is especially essential to create suppleness in the horse. Schooling without a rider on the lunge line or jumping in hand are often suitable means to accomplish this.

For horses with conformational flaws that move calmly and with rhythm, it is advisable to initially ride them in working speed, in rising trot, on long lines or large circles. Cavaletti, jumping, and climbing work under the rider are a suitable means for most horses to achieve suppleness, since—if done correctly—this work encourages the horses to arch the back upward and stretch the neck forward/down, even under less experienced riders.

The important point—whether on the lunge line or under the rider—is that the horse stretches the neck forward/down and that the lower neck line is never bent downwards [ewe neck]. The medium trot and all shortened [collected] working speeds, all turns and leg-yielding exercises, or tightening the rectangles are harmful, if ridden without flexion in the poll.

If it happens that the suppleness required for further schooling is not achieved by means of schooling on the lunge line or free jumping, nor by means of the described work under the rider, then those horses must be assigned to especially suitable riders, who are able to use their influence to relax the horse and put the horse on the bit as described in subparagraphs 14 and 15. Here, too, the core objective is to teach to horse to reach for the rider's hand, even when ridden by a less active rider later on.

X. Special Exercises.

54. General Remarks.

Special exercises form the transition from the actual riding education to the riders' and horses' full fitness for war duty. They must be incorporated into cross-country riding instruction early on.

55. Riding Cross-country in Full Marching Gear.

As soon as rider and horse somewhat securely manage cross-country rides, one can start with exercises with marching gear. While the exercises up to this point had mainly served the purpose of increasing the rider's riding skills and the overall development of the horse, the horses must now also be schooled to clear obstacles and climb under heavy dead weights.

Young riders must learn to assess what demands can be made on a fully packed horse, to carry their own equipment for the sake of

Bild 51.

Abrutschendes Pferd.

Figure 51: Sliding horse

their horse's well-being, mounting and dismounting quickly, and also to ride with a gas mask.

Skillfully navigating cross-country obstacles is essential for tactical mobility. The most common cross-country obstacles are **streams and artificial road blocks.**

One must utilize all opportunities that present themselves to cross **streams** by climbing. Whenever they are not present, one must be willing to accept longer detours.

The respective schooling must be expanded to an extent that even packed horses will willingly slide into **streams** with sloping embankments as long as climbing up the other side will not present considerable difficulties. In this regard, the packed horse is just about as capable as the lightly saddled horse.

If edges and ground of **ditches** allow, they must be climbed.

Especially in case of steep **inclines** that must be overcome uphill, and when jumping down onto hard roads in hilly terrain—particularly when riding in a unit—it may often be advisable to dismount and overcome the obstacle in hand.

Barricades in ravines or forested country roads must—whenever possible—be cleared by climbing closely around them in order to prevent having to take long detours.

56. Preparatory Exercises for Schooling in a Unit.

a) Working paces
Precondition for schooling in a unit is the ability to ride correctly at all paces. The steps per minute are: [The following definitions pertain to the listed paces and apply to the average Warmblood horse]:

At the walk	125 steps
- working trot	275 steps
- working canter about	500 steps (see following paragraph)
- extended canter about	700 steps (see following paragraph)

The normal pace at a canter on flat open terrain is 500 steps. In hilly open terrain with packed or fatigued horses, the pace can be decreased to 400 steps. The pace of the extended canter depends on the situation and type of terrain. Most of the time, it is up to the leader to

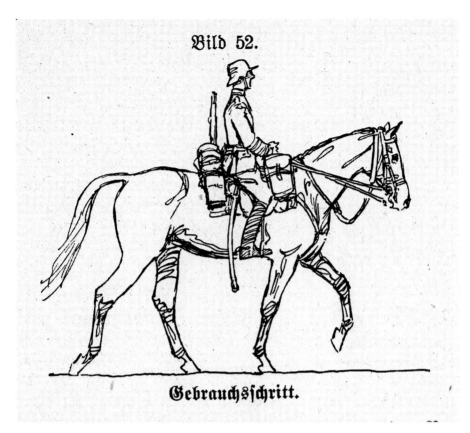

Bild 52.

Gebrauchsschritt.

Figure 52.

determine the pace, which is around 700 steps.

b) Transitions

All detachments must practice fluid transitions from march formation to queue, quick disbandment into a pack and forming a march formation, before beginning schooling in a unit. The horses must learn to perform these transitions habitually.

c) Leading of ponied horses and tying horses together

The rider is taught how to lead a ponied horse by leading one horse; only when the young rider can securely do so, will one progress to leading two or three ponied horses. For this purpose, the riders themselves must ride horses that are especially suited for the purpose. It therefore often becomes necessary to change horses for this duty. The rider ponying the horse(s) should not have to pay much attention to the horse that he is riding, so that he is able to keep his mind on the ponied horses and use calls and slow transitions to lead them into the movement, into a higher gait and vice versa.

Tying the horses together by means of coupling reins, head to the saddle, and having the rider, who is ponying the horses—and who must take care of a total of four horses—untie them is an exercise that must be practiced frequently in the cavalry.

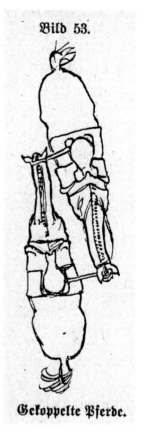

Bild 53.

Gekoppelte Pferde.

Figure 53.

57. Loading.

Smooth, trouble-free loading is precondition for quickly loading units onto a train. Since loading eight horses into one wagon can only be learned by practicing it, one must frequently create the respective opportunity for the young rider and the young horse. This must happen before they participate in war-like loading exercises in a larger unit, followed by transport.

This education is facilitated by creating a box without wheels in the size of a railroad car within the barracks, which can be used to practice loading.

58. Swimming with the Horse.
(Rescue service see All. P. D. subparagraph 492 [a different set of regulations].)

In order to quickly cross larger streams, it is necessary to instruct as many riders as possible in swimming with a horse.

Therefore one must demand that all riders who can swim will swim with a horse several times per year. For this purpose it is not sufficient to rely on the cross-country exercises held for larger units, where units ferry across streams. Instead, one must plan to conduct swimming exercises during individual training.

The individual rider must become so familiar with swimming with the horse that he learns to view the horse as a useful means to cross a stream. It is necessary to frequently practice how to quickly create makeshift rafts for weapons and equipment and how to carry them alongside the swimming horse.

One must undertake the following preparations for swimming with the horse:

The riders undress or at least take off jackets and boots, which are being ferried along with the saddles, the baggage, and the weapons. The horses are only bridled with a snaffle bit [no curb bit]. The snaffle reins are shortened by means of a knot and lie on the horse's neck, so that the rider stays independent of the rein and can hold on to mane or tail only.

When riding into the water, the rider grabs the knotted reins with both hands. As soon as the horse loses ground and willingly swims forward, the rider lets go of the reins and tightly grabs hold of the mane with his right hand, behind the rein and as closely as possible to the withers. At the same time, he slides off the horse to the left and lets the horse pull him along. For horses that swim slowly, it can be advisable to use the left hand and legs to help swim. In general, the rider must avoid lying over the horse with his body since this would put too much of a load on the horse's back. However, when the horse approaches the other side of the stream or possible sandbanks or shallows, where it can touch ground, the rider must position himself over the horse's back in due time so that he can get into the riding seat and can continue his ride.

If the mane is too short, one can use a stirrup leather—tied around the horse's neck—as an aid.

If the horse refuses and rears when riding into the water, the rider must hold on to the mane with one hand and to the knotted snaffle reins with the other. This helps prevent the rider from losing his seat on the bare horse, holding on to the reins, and flipping the horse over.

In order to keep horses swimming into the right direction, it is often enough to splash some water on the outside, otherwise very light sideways tugs on the inside snaffle rein. If the reins are pulled too strongly, the horse may easily topple over in the water.

With horses that swim securely and without much leg action, one can also hold on to the tail. In order to switch from the mane to the tail, the left hand grabs the mane, the right hand goes back to grab the tail, then the left hand lets go. In order to come back to the front, it suffices to perform a pull-up with the right hand until the rider's chest is above the horse's croup. Then the left hand reaches forward and grabs the mane, in order to pull the rider's body to the front again. Then the right hand grabs the mane again.

59. Weapons Training on the Horse.

Saber exercises [...] (H. Dv. 299/2).
Shooting pistols [...] (H. Dv. 240).

During all weapons drills, the rein hand must be placed firmly onto the crest. In order to quickly turn the horse towards all directions, one really has only weight and leg aids available. In order to familiarize the horses with weapons, this training must start early on.

60. Distance Rides of Individual Riders.

After the rider's education is completed, the rider must be required to **independently carry out a longer ride** (25 km/15 miles) across difficult terrain (partially at night) at a prescribed speed. It often depends on the successful completion of this training whether or not the expected results in the area of reconnaissance, delivery of messages, during marches, etc. are achieved.

Skillful and unhesitating cross-country riding, also when the rider is not being observed, proper assessment of the abilities of his horse and appropriate utilization of favorable terrain and ground conditions are essential for this purpose. Appropriate scheduling of the route, careful maintenance of the horse during breaks, and the ability to render first aid to a horse that suffered an accident or is injured, prevent the possibility that the horse's performance will be impaired.

The individual rider is usually ordered to complete the route that is to be ridden at a **prescribed speed**. This is either done by telling the rider by what time he must arrive at the destination or—for instance in case of messengers—by putting crosses on the message envelope.

While one cannot give any points of reference for open terrain with many obstacles, the following applies to flat open terrain and normal ground conditions:

X - one kilometer in 7-8 minutes or about 8 km/h, (5 mph)
XX - one kilometer in 5-6 minutes or 10 to 12 km/h, (6-7.5 mph)

The speed of 8 km/h can be maintained if the rider trots about 1/4 of the time and rides at the walk for the remaining time.

The speed of 10 km/h can be maintained if the rider trots a bit more than 1/2 of the time and rides at the walk for the remainder of the time.

The speed of 12 km/h (7.5 mph) can be maintained if one trots almost the entire time or if one canters about 1/4 of the time and rides the remainder of the time mostly at the trot, and occasionally rides at the walk. The rider rides this pace if he needs to ride short distances (2-3 km) (1.25-2 miles), otherwise only if he was told that the content of the message is especially urgent.

If the rider is on his own, he has the horse move calmly and in rhythm and chooses the pace for the respective gait that is most appealing to the horse. Extending or collecting this pace or any attempt to ask the horse to carry itself in a frame, other than the usual (working) frame, would result in excessive energy expenditure.

If time was lost, the rider should make up time by riding longer distances at the trot or by cantering, **never by increasing the pace.**

One does not change the hind leg to trot on during the individual trot distances. If—during a longer march—the horse shows that it is especially uncomfortable and fatiguing for it to have the rider trot on a particular hind leg, so that it practically seems to be lame, the rider must only trot on the hind leg that is comfortable to the horse. In order to be able to adhere to the commanded hourly speed, it is often necessary to trot downhill. Trotting uphill, however, should be avoided whenever possible.

If traffic considerations make it necessary, the rider will ride on the right side of the road. Otherwise he will chose the side of the road that is most comfortable to the horse. If the edges of the road are deep and uneven, it is preferable to stay on the center of the road, despite its hardness. This also applies to very convex paved roads.

61. Preparatory Training for Marches.

Long distance rides are also a good preparation for marching exercises. The preparation of bigger marches is usually scheduled during the time of unit training. Greater march efforts can only be undertaken without damaging the horse after previously conducting 3-4 weeks of marching exercises. At the core of the preparatory exercise is quiet marching work outdoors, 2-3 hours per day, mainly on hard roads. The marching speed is slowly increased to 7.5-10 km/h,(4.5-6.2 mph) depending on the respective objective. Once a week, the riders must go on an exercise march, which is 30 km (18.6 miles) in the first week and is increased during each following week by 10 km (9.3 miles) to a maximum of 74 km (46 miles). For these daily outputs, one must maintain a speed of 7.5 km/h (4.7 mph) on flat terrain, this includes short breaks.

The goal of the preparatory marching exercises is not only to increase the horse's performance, but also to increase the endurance of the rider when riding and leading, as well as his education in horse maintenance during the march, during breaks, and after reaching the destination.

The guidelines provided for individual riders in regard to assessment of roads, trotting downhill, etc. equally apply to marches. Maintaining a working pace is of greater importance during marches compared to the rides of an individual rider, where the horse picks the pace. During march exercises, the horses must be watered frequently. Before breaks—during which the horses are fed—the horses must be led or ridden in the walk until they have completely recovered.

Part C. Schooling of Horses.

XI. Dressage of Horses during the First and Second Year.

62. Goals and Principles of Dressage.

In order to be able to fulfill all requirements that military duty demands of a war-ready cavalry horse, the green horse's body needs to be systematically developed by means of gymnasticizing, and the horse needs to be carefully educated. Both elements combined are called dressage. The goal of dressage is to school the horse to the optimum performance level and to make it obedient. This goal can only be achieved if the horse—while maintaining and developing its natural [mental and physical] disposition—is brought into a form and posture in which it can fully develop its potential. In such form and posture, the horse will be able to prove equal to the demands of service for a long time.

a) The familiarization with the rider's weight

Dressage begins with starting the horse, whereby work on the lunge line and free lunging serve as preparatory means. Initially, the young horse should be prompted without a rider to release the tension created by the unfamiliar saddle and to become supple and unconstrained.

Then the young horse must learn how to carry the rider's weight, whose load places demands on the entire musculature of the horse, which it had previously been unaccustomed to. Especially the back, neck, and abdominal muscles used to stabilize the horse's horizontal spine must counteract the pressure of the rider's weight. In the green horse, they are often naturally not strong enough for this purpose. This correspondingly makes the horse stiffen its neck and back, rush forward, lean on the bit, stumble, and leads to other defects in posture and gait.

b) Rhythm, looseness

The rider's first task is to regulate the rhythm (see subparagraph 3). The horse goes in rhythm in the trot when the diagonal leg pairs are leaving and hitting the ground simultaneously and at a regular beat. Regulation of rhythm initially occurs in the natural trot, meaning at a pace that the horse in its natural posture will assume on its own without rushing. The horse must learn to regain the posture that it has found without rider and move just as unconstrained—with a long neck and a low nose—under the weight of the rider.

If it is able to maintain this unconstrained movement, it is 'loose' [looseness, "*Losgelassenheit*"]. Looseness is in evidence if the horse moves forward at the trot in rhythm, covering ground, without rushing, and wants to stretch the neck—nose reaching forward/down—towards the stationary hand, and it elastically swings in the back and carries the tail naturally without tension.

Looseness [*losgelassenheit*] of the horse is the basic precondition for the success of the entire dressage.

c) Development of impulsion and gait. Contact

The first aids that the horse must learn to obey are the driving aids. Obedience to these aids is the basis for the entire subsequent schooling of the horse. To begin, the pushing power of the hindquarters is developed by means of driving aids. The horse seeks contact with the rein, which results in a certain connection between the rider's hand and horse's mouth. This connection is called contact.

Contact must be the result of pushing power that was properly developed by means of driving aids. It must never be achieved by backwards action (pulling) on the reins.

The contact is correct when the horse gives the rider the feeling of a secure, soft connection between the hand and horse's mouth, when it stays on the leg without rushing, with rhythmic steps, and when its back swings in a way that enables the rider to stay in contact with the saddle in an erect, relaxed posture and drive. The degree of contact must initially always be decreased whenever there is a risk that the horse will lean on the bit, drag the hindquarters and lose the gait.

Once correct contact is established, one can improve the natural gait. In doing so, the legs should land on the ground rhythmically and push off the ground elastically. Forward movements should be energetic, yet effortless, never constrained and tense. The natural gait is facilitated by means of leg influences [aids], which prompt the hind legs to energetically push off and swing forward.

Here, too, the rider must always adjust his seat and movements to the horse, align his center of gravity with the horse's center of gravity and elastically swing with the horse's movement.

He feels clearly in both hands and under both seat bones that the work of the hindquarters is expressed by actively swinging back muscles in calm, steady, and energetic steps.

d) Straightening

With almost all young horses, there are difficulties in straightening. The reason is that horses are naturally crooked and narrower in the forehand than they are in the hindquarters. One result of this crookedness is uneven contact with the reins. This must be counteracted by driving the horse toward the loose rein, yielding with the tight rein and possibly holding the reins further apart (see subparagraph 29).

e) Through-ness. Yielding of the poll

As the horse is increasingly straightened, the horse's through-ness also improves. The push of the hindquarters can now work all the way [through the horse's body] into the horse's mouth without resistance. This causes the horse to yield to the pressure of the mouthpiece, yield in the poll and chew on the bit.

Thereby the horse slowly gains the ability to yield in the poll all on his own. **One must never attempt to achieve yielding in the poll by forcefully restraining neck and head. Instead, the ability to yield in the poll must be the result of the hindquarters pushing against the non-yielding hand.** This is the only way to achieve stabilization of the neck at the withers. Without this stabilization, a secure connection between forehand and hindquarters becomes impossible.

During schooling, it is never about working on individual parts of the horse's body; instead, it is always about the schooling of the entire horse. Difficulties and resistances—expressed by stiffness in the neck and poll, as well as in the back and the hindquarters—are always closely interrelated. The only way to overcome them successfully is movement. If the horse yields in the halt, the rider is easily deceived. Once he rides energetically forward, however, the rider's influence will be supported by the horse's needs to maintain its balance.

f) Development of carrying power. Collection

Once—during the first year of schooling—fresh forward movement and pushing power are sufficiently developed, a certain contact with the bit has been gained and a sufficient degree of throughness has been achieved, the dressage—in the following year—focuses on the task to make greater demands on the carrying power of the hind legs and therefore on collecting the horse.

An increased carrying power of the horse's hindquarters makes it possible to shift the center of gravity to the back, thus unloading the forehand, and increasing the load on the hindquarters. The horse's hindquarters are only able to carry more load, if they are able to flex in the joints under the load that is transferred onto them from the front while stepping forward [under the horse's body]. Increased flexion subsequently results in increased extension [of hindquarters/joints]. It is mainly this alternate flexing and extending of hind legs that makes this movement a gymnastic exercise.

Due to the increased activity of the hindquarters, the throughness is increased at the same time. Only if there is a completely secure line from back to front and front to back—not interrupted by any resistance on the part of the horse—can there be elastic counteraction between hindquarters and forehand, which alone makes correct collection possible. This also improves pace and impulsion. All exercises in bending and collecting work are closely interrelated. Here the horse learns to obey the interplay of the driving and restraining aids, as well as the inside and outside aids.

The muscles of the hindquarters, however, are not only strengthened by collecting exercises, but also by appropriate cross-country work and jumping exercises.

Constant change between cross-country work and work in the arena is the best way to prevent negative effects of incorrect collection.

100

Under no circumstances must the horse's natural gait and impulsion be impaired by collecting work.

g) Development of elevation

The more one succeeds in flexing the hindquarters during the course of this schooling and therefore make it more skilled in supporting and pushing the body weight, the stronger and more supple the muscles in back and hindquarters will become and the less will the horse search for support in the rider's hand and instead carry neck and head more or less high—depending on its conformation—meaning elevate itself.

There is no one neck and head posture that can be considered normal for all horses. One must rather find the posture that is most suitable for the individual horse's conformation. **The lower neck line must never be convex in shape forward-down [ewe neck].**

h) Working posture

The horse has this posture of neck and head—depending on the individual conformation of the horse—in the working posture. This posture is the rule. Here the horse—with energetically swinging, ground-covering steps and a swinging back, supple poll and neck, nose slightly in front of the vertical—should be on the bit with secure yet light contact and be in self-carriage while calmly obedient to the rider's aids. The rider, in turn, must have learned to use the correct interplay of aids to continuously re-establish the working posture if it gets lost. **The end goal is reached when the horse can easily be ridden in the working posture by an average rider and can be securely controlled when riding cross-country alone.**

Bild 54.

Gebrauchstrab (Reiter leicht trabend).

Figure 54. Working trot (rider posting the trot)

i) Dressage posture

The best posture of neck and head is when the neck freely rises from the withers and the upper part of the crest line forms a softly arched curve towards the poll, whereby the highest point is the poll; the head is carried in a way that its front edge—from forehead to nose—forms a perpendicular line. Such posture—dressage posture— enables the rider to have the best leverage effect on the hindquarters. At the halt and in collected gaits, however, the described degree of elevation and yielding of the poll must only be required of the horse for short periods of time. In more extended gaits, the rider must allow the horse to lengthen the curved neck and slightly move the nose forward [in front of the vertical].

102

A. Young Remounts.

(Dividing riders into detachments, subparagraph 96-101)

63. Treatment of a Young Horse.

The correct education of the young horses is critical for their eventual fitness [for duty]. Any cause for disobedience must be avoided in order to prevent fights with the rider. For the purpose of remediation of any occurring disobedience, the instructor's remedies provided in subparagraph 44 are of greater significance than those of the rider.

Careful, affectionate, and calm handling of the horse is just as important in the barn as it is during riding lessons.

Horses have a very well developed ability to remember praise and punishment. If the horse shows any sign of fear or excitement, one must initially attempt to have a calming influence. Some means of calming the horse are holding a food bucket, patting the neck, and the rider's calming voice.

64. First Saddling and Bridling.

Fitting of saddles and first saddling and bridling require special care and diligence. In the beginning, it is best to saddle the horse after it had the chance to move freely (subparagraph 65). At first, the saddle's girth is only tightened lightly and will only be tightened more after a longer break. The bridle is put on the horse while it is still standing at the manger.

One must pay continuous attention to the need to retighten the girth during work. In some young horses, it can be difficult to place the saddle in the proper position due to the fact that they do not carry their head and neck properly yet or have too big of a belly. In that case, one can use a foregirth until the horse has gained a better posture. A saddle that is positioned too far back is just as incorrect as a saddle that is too far forward. It is also wrong to tighten the girth too much and thus constrict breathing.

Equally important is to carefully select the proper bits right from the start. For horses that tend to put the tongue above the bit and stick it out of the mouth, one should tighten the noseband more.

Schooling Plan for Young Horses as a Guideline
FIRST YEAR (Young Remounts) – *First Semester*

	First work until mid-September	**October**
Suppling Exercises	Work on the lunge line	Stragglers work on the lunge line before or after the lesson. Jumping in hand up to 40 cm.
	Riding in a pack, initially behind a few lead horses.	
		Lengthening of the neck with nose pointing forward-downward
		Letting the horse chew the reins out of the hand under the rider.
		Individual horses, who offer to canter, canter for short periods of time.
Collecting Exercises		
Gaits and Tempi		
		Natural trot (rising trot), working trot, increasing speed in working trot and vice versa.
		Cantering of individual horses. See above.

November	December	January
Stragglers work on the lunge line before or after the lesson. Jumping in hand up to 40 cm.		
Mixed riding in a group with frequent change of direction.	Same as November	Same as November
Letting the horse stretch toward the bit with forward-downward pointing nose. Turns in motion and on the forehand.	Same as November	Same as November
First riding through corners.	Serpentines along the long side while bending under the rider. First in the walk then the working trot.	
Letting the horse chew the reins out of the hand under the rider.		
Stepping over ground poles.	Letting the horse chew the reins out of the hands in the walk and working trot to test the suppleness. Cavaletti work up to 15 cm in height.	Same as December
		First riding on a circle.
Walk on completely dropped reins.		Walk on the long rein.
Natural trot (rising trot), working trot, increasing speed in working trot and vice versa.		Same as December
Cantering with all horses.		Working canter on completely dropped reins.

Schooling Plan for Young Horses as a Guideline
FIRST YEAR (Young Remounts) – *First Semester cont'd*

	First work up to end of September	October
Transitions (only selected transitions are listed)		
Jumping and Field Training		Riding in a pack, in a line and in a group across uneven ground.
Education and Familiarization	Saddling and bridling.	Standing still when mounting, during all exercises.
Goals	Familiarization with the rider.	Rhythm, suppleness, no contact.

November	December	January
	Transition from walk to halt and move-off in the walk, from working trot to walk.	
Transition into canter by extending the working trot.		From the working trot to the walk and vice versa on the circle.
Riding in a pack, in a line and in a group across uneven ground.	Same as November	
Standing still when mounting, during all exercises.	Same as November	
	Standing still without contact when lining up.	
Riding with reins in one hand.	Same as November	
Beginning of contact, development of forward thrust and gait, straightening.	Same as November	

Schooling Plan for Young Horses as a Guideline
FIRST YEAR (Young Remounts) – *Second Semester*

	February	March
Suppling Exercises	Mixed riding in a group with frequent change of direction.	Jumping in hand up to 60 cm in height.
	Letting horse stretch down to the bit with forward-downward pointing nose.	Same as February
	Turns in motion and on the forehand.	Same as February
	Letting horse chew the reins out of the hand in walk, working trot and working canter to test the suppleness. First turns from the corner.	Same as February
Collecting Exercises	First application of half-halts.	Improvement of half-halts.

April	May	June	July to September
Jumping in hand up to 60 cm in height. Same as February		[This is what your horse should know now] Requirements: a.) Individual: Walk: Walk with completely dropped reins and on the long rein. Trot: Working trot	
Same as February Same as February First leg-yielding in the walk.	Same as February Same as February	with contact. 275x trot according to tempo markers. Rising trot. Canter: Working and medium canter on specific distances. In all three gaits: Letting horse chew reins out of the hand as a test to determine	
Improved riding through the corners and on the circle, increased aplication of the outside aids by yielding with the inside rein. Step forward and rein-back 1-2 steps.	Same as before. Turns in motion with tightening outside aids. Voltes first in the walk, then in the working trot*.	whether the horse stretches the neck forward-downward without rushing. Riding with reins in one hand. Halts, transitions, and turns at specific points. Jumping, climbing, familiarization with riding in the field and in [large groups].	

For driving horses: only those with special talent.

Schooling Plan for Young Horses as a Guideline
FIRST YEAR (Young Remounts) – *Second Semester cont'd.*

	February	March
Gaits and Tempi	Walk on the long rein.	
	Extension of working trot.	
	Working trot on a long and completely dropped rein.	Working canter.
Full Halts and Transitions (only selected ones are listed)	Halt from walk to halt and move-off in the walk. From the working trot to the walk and vice versa. Increase the working trot and vice versa. Halt from the working trot on the circle. Practice transitions and halts at specific points individually.	
Jumping and Field Training	Jumping under the rider across simple obstacles up to 50 cm high, trenches up to 1.50 m wide*.	
		Climbing on slopes, through water and through trenches, familiarization with terrain [field], riding in pairs at first, then individually according to markers.
Education and Familiarization	For the first time, standing still calmly with light contact in a group as well as individually at discretionary points in the arena, while other horses are in motion.	
Goals	Same as November through January	Improving contact, straightening, throughness & impulsion. Getting horse used to street noises.

April	May	June	July until September
Walk on the long rein.		[ct'd. This is what your horse should know now] b.) Riding with a group on a limited rectangle [arena]: June. Walk on a long rein. Working trot, changes of tempo, medium trot. Canter: working canter on 2 circles on both leads. Medium canter on long lines. In all 3 gaits, ride individual horses against the group and through the group. Line-up of the group in the walk. Horses calmly stand on a long rein...	Maintenance of the schooling level which has been achieved so far. Extending the working canter to the medium canter. Jumping in hand up to 1 m high in facilitating distances*.
Medium trot on short distances. Riding tempi by extending the working canter.	Medium trot on longer distances. 275x trot. Medium canter.		
Working canter on two circles.			
Halt from walk to halt and move-off in the walk. From the working trot to the walk and vice versa. Halt from the working trot on the circle. Practice transitions and halts at specific points individually.			
Same as February in the field.			
Climbing on slopes, through water and through trenches, familiarization with terrain [field], riding in pairs at first, then individually according to markers.			
Same as March. Brief riding in a group with distances in walk and trot.	Same as April. In the group: horses straight and with good alignment.		
Improvement of contact, straightening, through-ness and impulsion. Getting horse used to street noises.		Same as April-May	Same as April-May

For draft horses: only those with special talent.

111

65. Working on the Lunge Line and Free Lunging.

Initially, all horses must either be free-lunged or worked on the lunge line, using a lunge cavesson. The goal of this work is to encourage the horse to relax, to take even, calm steps, and to reach for the bit with the neck, nose pointing forward-down. This serves to supple and strengthen the back muscles and prepares them for carrying the load of the rider.

If the horses cannot be worked on the lunge line due to staff shortage, they can be exercised by free lunging, without lunge line or rider, for the purpose of achieving suppleness.

For this purposes, one prepares the arena as follows:

At a distance of 2.5 m, one creates a demarcation by means of poles or lines that are supposed to prevent the horses from running into the inside of the arena. Two calm, older horses under riders lead the way as guide horses. They are supposed to regulate the speed and prevent that the horses behind them break through and run forward.

Initially, the horses that are to be exercised are individually led by the bridle, reins in a knot and without side reins, at a distance of 1-2 m behind the guide horses, at the walk. After this has calmed them down a bit, they are let loose. The exercise is conducted at the walk and trot. During first couple of exercises, one must accept a certain level of agitation. After a few days, the horses can also be guided to freely move over ground poles or cavaletti. Once the horses have become used to this, one can soon begin free jumping (subparagraph 37). This is a good method to release the tension that was created by saddling and eliminate the friskiness after having been in the barn.

66. First Work under the Rider
(See subparagraph 62 a) and b)).

For young horses, it is desirable to achieve a **suitable, permanent rider/horse combination** as soon as possible. As soon as one anticipates, however, that a rider is not able to continue to develop his young horse, a change must take place.

For the first couple of days, the rider is lifted onto the horse when mounting. A helper grabs the rider's lower leg right below the knee with his right hand and lifts him up softly and quickly.

Initially it is advisable to start the horse under saddle in the **outdoor riding school** after lunge work or free lunging. One takes advantage of the horse's herd instinct and initially rides the young horses in a pack in the outdoor arena. It is advantageous to create a large, oval-shaped track, later a large figure eight.

When riding independently in a group in the arena, the horses can either go one behind the other or next to each other. Hot-tempered horses must continuously be taken out of the line and moved to the front. The key factor is individual work and exclusion of any avoidable force. One must certainly not demand from the riders to keep a distance [from the next horse].

One must ask **less of a work load** from horses that are weak, underdeveloped, still very much in the growth phase, and such horses that get hot easily. Lazy horses need more lively paces. Hot-tempered horses must be worked under especially supple riders in slower gaits

𝔅ilb 55.

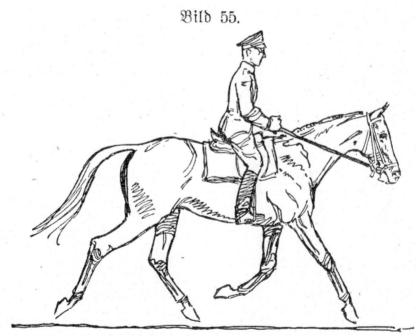

$\mathfrak{H}$altung der jungen Remonte beim erſten Anreiten
(Reiter leicht trabend).

Figure 55: Posture of the young horse when first started under saddle (rider posting the trot)

until they get less animated.

Coltish and fresh horses get as much work as needed, until they calm down and show signs of relaxation. Based on these facts, one determines the individual work load for every horse during every lesson. During the first couple of days, the horses stay under the rider for about 20 minutes. The rest of the lesson must be filled with other kinds of activities.

As soon as possible, and in any case before the young horse's strength is fully developed, one must go on ample **cross-country rides**. Here the horses must be ridden forward on long, straight lines. If the horses' accommodations are at an inconvenient location [for cross-country rides], they should be put on long side reins and be led out and back in hand next to old horses, and should be mounted once the open field is reached.

When first starting the horse under saddle, the rider does not wear spurs. Each remount rider carries a riding crop (about 1 m in length). Riding the green horse, the rider starts the preparatory driving aids by placing the riding crop at the inside shoulder. This aid can be increased up to light taps. If the rider cannot achieve the desired effect in this way, he lets the riding crop drop behind his leg against the horse's body. Gradually, the rider combines the use of the riding crop with increasingly noticeable taps from his lower leg. This makes the horse understand the driving leg aids.

In case individual horses continue to fight against the rider's weight by constantly hollowing the back, they should initially be ridden with **long side reins**. One must continuously make repeated attempts to make do without such reins. The initial short trot sequences on both reins primarily serve to encourage and also satisfy the horse's willingness to move and to also satisfy this willingness. In the process, the horse should find its rhythm and become supple.

In the beginning, one always **posts the trot**. The rider's main goal is to adjust to the horse's movement. The reins are held long, so that the bit does not cause the horse to feel discomfort on the bars. While striving to go with the horse's movement, the rider should often take the reins into one hand, grasp the pommel with the other hand and pull buttocks and legs well forward into the saddle.

One of the most important principles of schooling always remains to **encourage the horse to move forward boldly** and to maintain this tendency in the horse. The rider of a young horse must strive to rather ride the pace offered by the horse in a livelier fashion than to slow the pace down. At the same time, this serves to stretch the horse, which is an

114

essential precondition for straightening. The more one thinks of riding forward during this schooling phase and the less one influences the form of the horse by means of the hands, the better one succeeds in creating the basis for subsequent dressage.

If the horse offers the **canter,** one should accept it, assume a light seat and position the hands low without pressing down, so that the horse can freely execute the canter strides. Out of consideration for the still soft joints and muscles of the horse, one should, however, refrain from longer canter stretches during this phase.

In order to transition down to the **walk** at the end of the first trot exercises, the rider closes his knees more tightly, slightly tilts the upper body to the front and brings his horse to transition down into the trot by applying several asking and yielding rein aids. Once the horse has transitioned into the walk, the rider sits and immediately completely gives the rein (walk see subparagraph 71).

As soon as the horses are familiar with the driving aids, one can start **working with cavaletti**. For the young horse, the main value of cavaletti work is in suppling the tense back musculature of the horse and in achieving correct activity of the back. Cavaletti work is executed at the walk and trot, i.e. initially posting the trot over a few ground poles. Only when the horse has become used to stepping over these poles in rhythm can one increase the number and height of cavaletti. In the process, the horses learn how to lengthen their necks and to stretch. The hindquarters are activated and strengthened. The rider must unload the horse's back somewhat without coming out of the seat and must supply follow the horse's movements. One must often practice **mustering** during and at the end of the riding lesson; initially, the main focus should simply be on having the horse stand still without requiring contact or alignment.

In order to make the horse familiar with the effect of the reins and also teach him to trust the bit, one can start practicing **letting the horse chew the bit in hand** (subparagraph 51).

67. Beginning Contact, Transitions, Working Trot.
(Subparagraph 62 c)

In the beginning, the horse must only go in **contact** for short periods of time since otherwise, there is the risk that the horse will lean on the bit, drag the hindquarters, and lose the gait.

Once the horse stretches the neck and searches for the bit, however, one must allow contact for a short period of time. Right from the start one should strive for even contact in order to straighten the horse.

Once the horse has found a slight contact in the natural trot and carries the rider with swinging back, the moment has come to develop a **working trot** from the natural trot. Frequently increasing speed on shorter stretches awakens the horses' desire for bold forward movement—meaning the willing forward movement that is so important for schooling—and develops pushing power in the hindquarters.

Such work causes the horse to become lazier—especially towards the end of the riding lesson—and the horse will want to be encouraged to move forward. The rider can now also **sit the trot** for short periods of time.

Those horses that seemingly are easy to ride, **curl up their neck** and prematurely give the rider the feeling of substantial yielding in the poll and elevation, require special attention. For these horses, one must repeatedly drive the nose in front of the vertical. Otherwise, there is a risk for development of a false bend in the neck. Once established, this type of bend is hard to remediate. The lower neck line must never be bent forward [ewe neck]. Having the riders frequently ride with one hand, moving the rein hand forward while maintaining contact, are the best methods for preventing the risk that the horses become too short in the neck.

Yielding rein aids are a good touchstone for checking the correctness of the work. Here, the rider lets the horse "chew" the rein out of his hands without abandoning the driving aids. While doing so, the horse must move in a fully relaxed fashion without rushing, stretching his neck forward, with a slightly arched crest line and nose pointing forward-down.

If the horse does not show a stretch in the neck musculature in response to this relief or if it takes the reins out of the rider's hand with a sudden movement, these are clear proofs that neck and back musculature is not yet supple; in almost all cases, this means that the rider has worked with too much hand influence and too little driving aids. After some time, it must be possible to effortlessly reestablish contact with the reins. These yielding rein aids must also frequently be used when riding cross-country.

116

Once the horses have learned to respond to the **leg aids** by moving forward without losing contact, the rider's legs gradually start influencing the horse during transitions, in a way that encourages it to step under more with its hind feet. The rider now also requires the horse to stand straight. If it evades to the back or sides, it will be straightened in a forward movement. For this purpose, the rider rides forward a few steps against the light, carried hand (work at the walk, see subparagraph 71).

68. Obedience to the Unilateral Aids.

a) Riding through corners and turns

In the beginning, the arc through the corner must be ridden flat enough not to disturb free forward movement. The inside hand remains in position, the outside hand yields, the inside leg—at first in a tapping movement, later by adhering to the horse's body—maintains the flowing forward movement. After riding through the corner, the rider carefully reinstates the effect of the outside rein by yielding with the inside rein. Both legs, mainly the inside leg, drive the horse forward and now towards both reins. These aids are to be used for all turns during movement, respectively.

As the musculature of the hindquarters continues to strengthen, the horse is increasingly pushed into the corner (subparagraph 21, 22).

b) Turns on the forehand

Even though the turn on the forehand is not a proper schooling lesson, it nevertheless provides the easiest means of teaching the young horse obedience to the unilateral rein and leg aids, since one can mechanically drive the horse into this turn (also see subparagraph 20).

c) Serpentines on the long side and bending under the rider

At first, the curve is ridden on the long side in a very flat arc. As the horse's softness in response to the increase of inside aids, one can increase the arc towards the inside of the arena. If the necks are sufficiently stabilized at the withers, one can incorporate "bending under the rider" (subparagraph 30).

At first, the exercise should be performed in the walk, then in the working trot.

During the first year, bending under the rider should only be practiced carefully and for brief periods of time while riding forward energetically. Otherwise, there is the risk that the horses become loose in the neck and too short [in the neck]. After bending, the horses must again always be ridden in free gaits towards both reins [on the bit].

d) Riding circles and voltes

Riding on a circle is beneficial and can be started once the horses have gained contact on a straight line. Even though it is not yet possible at this point to make the horse's body align exactly with the arc of the circle and to bend it respectively, riding on a circle does encourage the horse to step forward more with the inside hind foot and makes the horse more agile. The best way to start this is to ride a large circle outdoors.

Once the horses have learned to stay on the arc of the circle, one can move on to practicing the volte, initially only in the walk. Here, the diameter of the volte must be determined by the degree to which the horse can bend; the diameter must be greater than 6 stides [meters].

e) Leg-yielding

Leg-yielding must only be practiced at the walk. It is beneficial to prepare this exercise by practicing lateral movements [crossing over] in hand (subparagraph 52).

One can start leg-yielding once the horse is familiar with the use and effect of the unilateral rein and leg aids and is properly ridden towards both reins. Since there is the risk that the young horses will lose their eagerness for forward movement, posture and gait, and are easy to come behind the bit, leg-yielding should be limited to a few steps (subparagraph 31).

69. Using the Medium Trot to Improve Gait and Through-ness.
(See subparagraph 62e)

Once the horse's muscles—especially croup, back, and abdominal muscles—are sufficiently developed and the pushing power of the hindquarters as well as the carrying ability of the back have been established, one can start asking for more secure contact.

From this point in time on, one must use the medium trot to improve the gait and the ability to yield in the poll, while increasing the use of the hindquarters.

The medium trot is the best touchstone for checking whether schooling was properly structured. At the same time, it is the best way to remediate mistakes that were created through incorrect collection. Precondition is, however, that one does not lose the horse's ability to yield in the poll. Without this ability, the medium trot prevents any progress in dressage.

When working in the medium trot, one must take the individual horse's talents into special consideration. In the beginning, one should only demand a few steps, then increase the demand gradually. For horses with a weak back, the rider must post the trot when initially riding the medium trot.

In order to achieve the medium trot, the horses are increasingly driven towards the even, non-yielding reins—if needed with the aid of a riding crop. If the horse starts rushing when speeding up, if it takes uneven steps or carries head and neck too high while back activity is lacking, the rider slows the speed down and will only increase it again when the long, calm steps and a certain level of yielding in the poll have been reestablished.

In the process, the rider must strive to keep his horse straight. The eagerness to move forward and the contact that was already established must not be lost. If this happens anyway, the horse must initially be allowed to move in a crooked posture, that suits the horse more, until one overcomes the unilateral resistance in poll and hindquarters.

70. Beginning Collection.

By means of contact, the horse is already framed in a low-grade collection between the weight, leg, and rein aids. This grade of collection depends on the conformation and disposition of the horse and on the rider's skills. In general, the horse's mouth will be about at hip height, in horses with a low-set neck and long, weak, back, somewhat below that line.

The first beginnings of collecting work after developing the medium trot consist of rhythmic collection of the working trot, which must only be demanded for a few steps. Furthermore, it consists of stepping towards the outside aids, improving the way one rides through corners and on a circle (subparagraph 22, 23). In the process, one must ensure that the horse's neck remains fixed at the withers on curved lines and that the degree of bend in the horse's neck and poll does not exceed the degree of bend in the rest of its spine. One must frequently yield with the inside rein while simultaneously increasing the driving aids with the inside leg.

a) Turns during movement

The best way to prepare the horses for turns with [circle] reducing outside aids, is bending as well as work on the circle and the volte with expanded track. One begins by riding a half circle and back to the track out of the second corner of the long side. By increasing application of the outside aids, the arc is slowly reduced.

b) Rein-back

Rein-back improves through-ness. It is best prepared by practicing in hand work without rider. If the horse willingly yields to the pressure of the bit during this exercise, the exercise can be performed under the rider. The rider slightly tilts the upper body forward; he must ensure that he does not get stuck pulling the reins and initially be satisfied if the horse takes one or two steps back. The horse must be praised after every execution.

c) Halts

One can only demand correct halts after the young horse has been made sufficiently supple by means of half-halts in various transitions in the trot and canter. During the first year, one should only demand a halt from the walk. After every halt, the rider must yield the reins and praise the horse. (subparagraph 27).

71. Walk.

The walk, if properly ridden, is an especially good way to work the young horse, it calms it down and gets it used to the rider's driving aids.

Initially, the young horses must be ridden at a completely loose rein until their walk is completely calm and even and covers a lot of ground. Only then can one strive for slight contact. Even then, one must

Bilb 56.

Schritt der jungen Remonte mit geringer Anlehnung.

Figure 56: Walk of a young remount with slight contact

refrain from asking the horse to yield in the poll (figure 56).

Many riders attempt to shape the neck in the walk, especially during breaks. This significantly damages the ability to step forward and the ability to flex in the haunches and must therefore not be done.

72. Canter.

The canter contributes significantly to the improvement of suppleness. Many horses become supple better and quicker in the canter than in the trot. Riding instructors and rider must recognize and take advantage of this fact without overexerting the horse (subparagraph 66).

As soon as the horses have learned to relax their back in the natural trot and to carry the rider's weight without rushing—also in the bend offered by rounding the corners—one can start with the actual canter work.

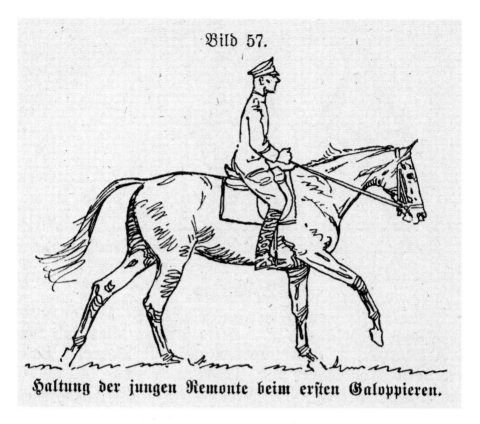

Bild 57.

Haltung der jungen Remonte beim erſten Galoppieren.

Figure 57: Posture of the young horse during the first transition into the canter

The canter is developed by speeding up the trot. This is easiest on a large circle outdoors. In the enclosed arena, it is developed on a circle line, in the direction towards the kicking board.

Initially, the canter aids are supported by tapping the riding crop against the inside shoulder and clicking of the tongue. The hands let the canter stride out by yielding the reins.

Many horses evade the aids by transitioning into an extended trot. In that case, the rider must first lead his horse back into a calmer pace. Only then can he reapply the canter aids.

On horses with weak backs and bad lumbar area, as well as horses with weak hindquarters, the rider must initially push his hip well forward and tilt his upper body forward in order to absorb the horse's awkward movements and to be able to unload the hindquarters.

One should initially allow these horses a certain amount of stronger contact, with neck in a low position. As the horse's back continues to get stronger, the rider must sit up again and utilize the driving aids to reduce the contact to a normal level.

The rider must strive for a natural, calm stride that cannot be reduced or expanded until later [in the schooling]. Initially, one must only canter for short periods of time. To end the canter, one lets the horse transition into the working trot and only then into the walk.

In order to steady the young horse on the respective inside foot in the canter, one gradually increases the time that one canters on the same rein. By repeatedly transitioning into the canter, the horses learn how to easily pick up the correct canter lead and this will gradually create a certain steady pace, the working canter.

In open terrain, one must practice cantering across even, later across uneven ground, then practice cantering uphill and downhill.

The medium canter is the pace closest to the working canter and the pace that is most suitable to develop the pushing power and springiness, as well as the suppleness of the horse. Medium canter is gradually developed from the working canter by riding long lines outdoors while increasingly driving the hindquarters forward. At the end of the first schooling year already, one should ride stretches of service canter on long lines outdoors. This strengthens the horse's heart and lungs.

73. Jumping.

One must strictly differentiate between jumping the horses in hand for the purpose of increasing the jumping ability, and jumping for the purpose of achieving suppleness (subparagraph 65). Jumping horses in hand must therefore not be practiced until the horses are supple, meaning in the middle or at the end of a lesson.

Once the horses have learned to jump securely, one can start jumping under the rider. In the beginning, one always jumps behind secure lead horses, in order to prevent any kind of disobedience. Jumping with a supple back especially benefits the gymnastic training of the horse.

74. Work in Open Terrain and Education.

In open terrain, horses must first be ridden forward in a pack, then in pairs, later individually at the walk on a loose rein and at the working trot on long lines. First they are ridden on roads and paths, then across even, later across uneven ground. The horses must also be taught jumping skills in open terrain by jumping behind lead horses and in a group (subparagraph 42).

One must attach special importance to the education of the young horse. The horse must learn to stand quietly in open terrain—alone as well as in proximity of other moving horses—especially during mounting and dismounting. The herd instinct—which is initially utilized to develop willing forward movement—must later be continuously combated.

At first, turns into the direction of the barn must only be performed at the walk.

One must use a methodical approach to get the horses used to street noise and troop service.

B. Schooling of the Horses in the Second Year
(Subdivision into detachments see subparagraphs 96-101.)

75. Work during the First Few Weeks. Medium Trot.

By now, the horses have gained strength and must be increasingly driven towards the outside aids by extensive work on circles in shortened working trot and canter. Continuous change of pace between medium and working trot on the circle and going large as well as backing increase the responsiveness to half-halts, and therefore the hindquarters' through-ness and ability to flex. Leg-yielding improves the obedience to leg aids. Enlarging and tightening the rectangle are proven methods to make horses supple and obedient.

Gradually, one should use longer stretches of medium trot to solidify rhythm and pace. The medium trot must be ridden after every collecting exercise. An especially educational sequence of exercises is to ride the medium trot after the shortened working canter, since the latter is best suited to prepare the hindquarters' ability to flex. If individual horses then step forward with a lot of impulsion and they

Bild 58.

Mitteltrab.

Figure 58: Medium trot

stay securely on the bit without leaning on it, one can extend the pace above that of the medium trot for a few steps at a time with these horses. However, as soon as the horse rushes and steps on its own feet, one must slow the pace down.

76. Collecting Exercises.
(See subparagraph 62 f) and g))

The precondition for collecting work is obedience to the outside aids.

In order to increase the horse's attention and obedience to the outside rein(s), one practices riding in position and outside position at the walk and shortened working trot; the work in outside position especially compels the horses to be obedient to the outside aids (subparagraph 33).

Schooling Plan for Young Horses as a Guideline
SECOND YEAR (Old Remounts)

	October	November
Suppling Exercises	Jumping in hand up to 80 cm high on both long sides of the arena.	
	Work over cavaletti in the working trot. Letting the horse chew the reins out of hand and pick them back up in the working trot and working canter.	
	Leg-yielding, serpentines, turns in motion.	Enlarging and tightening the rectangle in the walk and working trot. Letting horse chew reins out of the hands, in hand.
Collecting Exercises	Transition to canter from the working trot and walk.	Transition to canter from the walk and shortened working trot from the volte.
	Exact riding on the circle and through the corner.	
		Enlarging and tightening the circle, initially in the walk, the same in outside flexion and in shortened working trot.
		Turn on the haunches
		In-hand work: letting horse step forward and back in hand.

December	January	February	March
Same as November	Same as November		
Same as November			
Same as November	Same as November		
Transition to canter from the walk and shortened working trot on the circle and at discretionary points on the large track.	Improved transition into canter, as before, also canter move-off from the halt.		
Same as November	Counter canter on long sides, frequent canter lead changes*, change through the circle in the shortened working trot. Turning with and without change of flexion. Half-pirouette in walk*. Shoulder-in*.		
Leg-yielding with approach towards shoulder-in.	Improved volte in the shortened working trot.		Individual horses in the volte in collected canter*.
Same as November		Rein-back up to 4 steps.	
Stepping forward and back under the rider, 2-3 steps.			

For carriage horses: only those with special talent.

127

Schooling Plan for Young Horses as a Guideline
SECOND YEAR (Old Remounts) – *cont'd.*

	October	November
Gaits and Tempi	Walk on the long rein, working trot, medium trot. In the field working trot, working canter, medium canter.	Development of the shortened working trot and working canter.
Full Halts and Transitions (only selected ones are listed).	From the free walk on a long rein to the halt and move-off again.	From the working trot to the halt and trot-off again.
	From the working trot to the walk on the long rein.	From the medium trot to the collected working trot and back.
	From the working canter to the working trot and canter-off again.	From the working canter via a few trot steps to the walk on a long rein.
	Extending the working canter and vice versa.	

December	January	February	March
Shortened working trot and working canter. 500x—canter. Walk on the bit, otherwise as in October.	Extending the medium trot with individual horses. Otherwise as in December.	Same as January	
From the lengthened working trot to the halt.	From the medium trot to the halt.		
From the medium trot to the walk on the bit.		Same as December and January	
Same as November			
Same as November, but to the walk on the bit.		From the shortened working canter to the walk on the bit.	

Schooling Plan for Young Horses as a Guideline
SECOND YEAR (Old Remounts) – *cont'd.*

	October	November	December
Jumping and Field Training	Cantering across uneven ground. Easy slope jumps. Schooling horse in securely jumping off over several light jumps.	Jumping in hand up to 1 m high*.	Same as November up to 1.20 m high*.
		Jumping over simple, double, and spread obstacles with facilitating distances, trenches of up to 2.50 m*. Jumping under the rider up to 1 m high*.	
Education and Familiarization.	Mixed riding in a group. Familiarization with streets and [large number of horses].	Mixed riding in a group.	Individual tasks.
Goals	Suppleness, decisive contact.	Suppleness, straightening, impulsion, beginning collection.	Same as November.

* For carriage horses: only those with special talent.

January	February	March
Same as December		
In addition, two to three times per week brief riding in a group. Double bridle.		
Same as November and December, improved collection.		

Bild 59.

Schulterherein.

Figure 59: Shoulder-in

Riding in outside position also serves as a preparatory exercise for the counter canter (subparagraph 19).

As the through-ness of the horse increases, the rider practices the full halts, also from the trot and canter (subparagraph 27).

As soon as the horses can be led through the corners in good collection, stay securely on the outside aids and know how to turn on the haunches, one can start practicing the half-pirouette at the walk (subparagraph 26).

One can ride the shoulder-in as soon as the horses have gained the ability for through-ness, self-carriage, and yielding in the poll at the shortened working trot. Initially, the shoulder-in should only be practiced for brief periods of time at the walk for the purpose of educating rider and horse. One should soon transition into the shortened working trot so that eagerness and impulsion will not be diminished. This will also prevent the riders from pulling the horse together too much in the walk. Especially when ridden on the right rein, the shoulder-in increases flexibility, throughness, and straightening (subparagraph 34).

The transitions from "shoulder-in at the shortened working trot" to the medium trot as well as the shortened working canter and back are especially educational.

Based on the collecting work, the horse will be enabled to be temporarily ridden in dressage posture for short periods of time at the end of the second year of schooling (subparagraph 62 i).

77. Walk.

Gradually, one must achieve a firmer contact than with the young remount [horse during the first year of schooling], but only under

Bild 60.

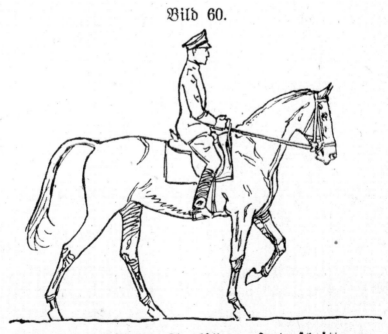

Schritt eines in der Ausbildung fortgeschrittenen
Pferdes im 2. Jahr.

Figure 60: Walk of a horse advanced in its schooling during the second year

the precondition that [the increased contact] does not disturb the quiet, ground-covering, and steady footfall.

The walk must be eager and active, it must not be ambling [lateral, pace-like]. Horses that take short steps will be given a longer rein and increasingly driven forward by means of leg aids, even if the horse takes a few trot steps as a result. Here, one should incorporate trot and canter exercises. If a horse rushes forward, the rider must try to hold the horse back by means of half-halts without starting to pull. Gradually, the contact becomes firmer, the rein a bit shorter.

Even in the second year, the walk must be extensively practiced. In order to make the walk more ground-covering, one must also repeatedly practice walk on a loose rein with horses during the second year.

78. Canter.

In order to shorten [collect] the working canter, one often transitions into the canter. It is harmful to shorten [collect] the canter strides during the working canter itself.

It is also especially beneficial to transition into the canter out of a shortened working trot, right after enlarging the circle after having first tightened the circle.

One must ensure that the horse also shows steady and lively strides during the shortened working canter. It must be encouraged by continuously driving with the inside leg.

The horse must not be required to transition into the canter on a straight line until it has learned to carry itself in the canter. Transitioning into the canter when riding in a detachment [group] while going large must not be required before the end of the second year. Frequent changes of lead in the canter at a shortened working pace makes the horses especially agile. Counter canter must only be practiced with individual horses.

It is necessary to frequently change the rein as well as alternately riding on a circle and going large, and alternate between working canter and medium canter. If canter stride sequences cease to be lively at the

Bild 61.

Verkürzter Arbeitsgalopp.

Figure 61: Shortened [collected] working canter

shortened working canter, one must ride at a freer pace from time to time.

From the beginning, one must also pay attention to straightening the horse in the canter. This is also the best way to prevent the horse from positioning the hindquarters towards the inside of the arena, a problem that is usually caused by pulling on the inside rein and lack of activity of the inside leg.

Move-off into the canter must also be practiced from the halt. For this purpose, the hind feet must be lined up well. In the beginning, one should allow the horse to take one step forward before moving off into the canter.

79. Work in Open Terrain. Education. Jumping. Special Exercises.

The cross-country schooling that was already started with the horse must now be methodically improved. Frequent cross-country exercises across uneven ground, jumping uphill and downhill across hill jumps, climbing and swimming do not only strengthen the muscles of the hindquarters, but also teach the horse to trust its own ability to perform and make the horse secure. Special exercises (paragraph X) prepare the horse for military service.

80. Military Service of Horses in the Second Year.

The objective is to incorporate as many horses in their second year as possible into the troops at the height of their strength and liveliness. During this first year at the front it is also necessary to handle them gently and provide them with special care so that the horses will not wear out prematurely. On occasion, riding horses need rework.

It is allowed to take fully developed horses in their second year to the big troop exercises and the fall exercises if the detachment commander gives the respective order. In the cavalry, however, they must still be spared strenuous exercises. In other forces, they must not be used as saddle horses [in a team, left side of the pole] but instead as lead or riding horses.

Part D. Schooling of the Rider.

XII. Recruits.
(Subdivision into rider detachments)

81. Assigning Horses to Recruits.

The most important basis for the schooling of the recruits is to assign the appropriate horses.

It is desirable to have enough horses available for the schooling of recruits to make it possible for every recruit to have his own horse. Assigning horses in this way also benefits the continued schooling in other service branches and in open terrain.

Recruit horses [school horses] must be checked in regard to their suitability for this special purpose before the recruits arrive [at the school] and should be reworked for this purpose, if necessary. One important aspect is that the horses move calmly and chew on the bit [accept the bit] when equipped with side reins. Individual horses must be worked on the lunge line. Later—especially when the recruit learns the interplay of aids—one must strive to have good riders frequently work the school horses before the recruit riding lessons. In doing so, the older rider will become an assistant instructor to the individual recruit.

Frequently changing horses during the duration of schooling is not only helpful when trying to find the appropriate horse for the individual recruit, but also helps achieve an improvement in his skills by having to adjust to horses with different temperaments.

School horses that the rider is not able to independently ride in self-carriage must be ridden in side reins so that the horses relearn how to give to the bit and the recruit gains the feel for a properly moving horse. The side reins are adjusted long enough to prevent the horse from pushing the underside of the neck forward [inverted neck]. The sooner they can be eliminated, the better. Side reins must never be used when riding walk at the end of the lesson or when jumping.

82. The Course of Schooling.

(See plan page 140).

Since the recruit—in addition to being schooled as a rider—must be educated as a soldier at the same time, he must be monitored and observed more than older riders. Saddle sores and accidents can be prevented by CARE. In the beginning, the riding lesson must be interrupted by frequent breaks.

The recruit also requires frequent verbal individual instruction in the basic concepts of riding and during the individual exercises.

From the start, one should place special emphasis on those exercises that are suited to make the rider supple, self-confident, agile, and alert. Among those are:

Agility exercises on the live horse,
Calisthenics,
Cavaletti work,
Jumping,
Saddling and unsaddling,
Coupling of horses [tying horses together head to saddle],
Mounted speech exercises in all gaits.

As soon as the recruits have gained a certain level of security in their seat (no later than after the second week), some of the riding lessons must be conducted in open terrain, where one will have the opportunity—especially in the fall—to extend the riding lessons to several hours of calm work and to combine it with other types of schooling. Longer work in the saddle will be the fastest way to make the young rider confident and secure. One then soon begins with "Special Exercises" in open terrain (see paragraph X).

Also during those months when weather conditions dictate that one primarily uses the indoor arena, the recruits must ride cross-country, at least once per week for several hours.

Jumping must be conducted in a fashion that will—as much as possible—prevent any falls. One starts with preparatory

138

jumping exercises only when the horses have become completely supple so that the recruit is able to drive during the jump. For recruits, one must place even greater value on the use of lead horses in open terrain, on correct measurements and inviting obstacle design, as compared to other divisions.

Plan for Schooling Recruits in the Winter as a Guideline

	October	November
Attire, Equipment.	Riding suit without spurs, sports suit during agility exercises. Horses in snaffle and with side reins.	Same as October, sometimes with spurs, horses sometimes without side reins.
Seat exercises, Calisthenics, and Agility Exercises.	Agility exercises on the live horse. Jumping on and off, calisthenics, speech exercises.	
	In the halt, walk, and canter.	Same as October, also in the trot.
Gaits, Exercises on an Even Track [Flat Work].	Walk without stirrups. Canter without stirrups. Rising trot with stirrups, starting in the middle of the month, also trot without stirrups. Transition into the canter from the walk and trot on a large circle.	Walk without stirrups. Canter and trot without stirrups. Turns on the forehand. Transitions into the canter from the trot.

December	January	February	March
Same as November.	Double bridle.	Double bridle. Sometimes in full marching gear.	Same as February.
Same as November.	Occasional repetitions.	Same as January.	Same as January.
Same as October, also over cavaletti in the trot.			
Sitting the trot with stirrups for the first time. Walk with stirrups. Canter without stirrups. Leg-yielding at the walk. Starting to give aids. Transitions into the canter from the trot. Full halt from the walk. Frequently letting the horse 'chew the reins out' of the hand.	Riding with stirrups. Speeding up from the working trot and working canter. Transition into the canter from the walk in a volte. Full halts from the trot.	Repetitions. Backing. Medium trot. Medium canter. Transition into the canter from the walk after the corner.	Repetitions. Half-pirouettes at the walk. Turn on the haunches. Repeatedly transition into the canter from the walk.

Cont'd.

	October	November
Work Over Cavaletti, Jumping, Cross-Country Riding. **Special Exercises.**	Riding over ground poles in the walk and trot. Riding over cavaletti in the walk and trot without stirrups and with side reins. Riding in a pack in the walk and trot with stirrups.	Same as October, plus: Light climbing, riding across uneven terrain in a pack in the walk and trot with stirrups. Jumping, no more than 1.5 m high and small ditches behind lead horses. Riding over cavaletti at the trot with and without stirrups.
Goal*		Complete suppleness.

142

December	January	February	March
Same as October, plus: Riding over cavaletti without side reins. Cantering in a pack. Climbing and individual riding in the walk and trot across uneven ground. Individual jumping. 0.5 m and small ditches. Riding through water behind lead horses. Riding different tempi in the walk and trot.	Same as December, plus: Cantering alone. Riding in slippery and snow conditions. Transitioning from marching order to pack and back. Riding different tempi in the canter.	Same as January, plus: Jumping uphill and downhill, hill jumps no more than 0.5 m high. Individuals ride away from a dense pack. Sliding down inclines and into shallow water. Distance rides from 5 to 10 km. Riding in full marching gear and wearing gas mask. Weapons exercises. Horse holder duty.	Same as February, plus: Canter through the forest uphill and down hill*. Extended canter. Individuals jump small open-water jumps of 0.8 m*. Distance rides with obstacles, 10-15 km. Ride alone at night.
Supple seat, correct application of aids, mastering the horse in the previously learned exercises.		Perfecting the seat and mastering of the horse when riding alone.	

If draft horses are assigned to recruits, only if these horses are especially suited to do so.

83. Seat Exercises and Calisthenics.

These exercises are a good method to teach a young rider a relaxed seat that is independent of the rein and to eliminate a bad seat. They must be practiced at a calm pace in a closed detachment [one rider behind the other], for not too long periods of time. The reins must be knotted in such a way that the rider will have immediate contact with the horse's mouth once he grasps the reins. The first rider keeps the reins in his hands. One must prevent riders from falling off the horse.

The following exercises can serve as a guideline:

a) For the purpose of improving the seat:

Lifting the leg sideways and back with bent knee, while the tips of the feet hang loosely. This exercise must always come from the foundation, the buttocks; for this purpose, the upper body should be erect and rest on the buttocks, the thighs should be lifted—from the hip joint—as far out and back as needed to have the thigh and lower leg touch the horse with the flat inside, while the knee is bent and elastic.

Lifting one leg and turning the thigh from the hip joint; then pushing the leg back from the hip joint, while the flat inside of the leg touches the horse. The tips of the feet hang down loosely.

b) For the purpose of strengthening the leg and back muscles:

Bending the trunk back, as far as possible, without changing the leg position, meaning not moving the thigh forward. This exercise must only be performed in the halt and walk and is increased until the rider is able to lay his back down on the horse's back.

c) For the purpose of gaining an independent seat and making the hip joint flexible:

(Hands in riding position) bending head and trunk sideways and forward; turning head and trunk, rolling head and trunk, swinging both arms at the same time in large circles (as far back as possible and without losing adherence in the riding seat).

144

d) For the purpose of independent mobility of lower legs and feet:

Moving the lower legs from the knee joint forward and back while keeping the thighs as stretched and quiet at the horse as possible, and keeping heels low; rolling the feet.

A good exercise for obtaining a supple balanced seat is throwing and catching of items such as a ball or hat at the walk and quiet canter, later at the trot and during cavaletti work.

84. Agility Exercises on the Live Horse.

These serve to enhance the rider's agility. If possible, they must be practiced with all recruits. During practice, the recruit wears a sports suit, except in cold weather.

Horses that are suitable for the purpose of agility exercises on the horse are medium sized horses with a good saddle area, strong legs, calm temperament, but with go.

The equipment includes:

A vaulting roller, lunge cavesson, snaffle, side reins, lunge line, long whip.

The horse must also be accustomed go on the lunge line without side reins.

For one hour of practice with a detachment one requires two horses that take turns, since a horse should not canter continuously more than 20 minutes on the lunge line.

One starts with exercises in the walk and trot, but then quickly transitions to the canter.

For the purpose of mounting the moving horse, the rider takes hold of the two handlebars from the top, stays close to the horse's body, picks up the horse's gait, then pushes off with both legs and slides into the riding seat. The faster the horse moves, the further forward the rider must jump off and pull against the movement with bent arms, so that he won't land too far back on the horse or on its other side.

Bild 62.

Gewandtheitsübungen am lebenden Pferd.

Figure 62: Agility exercises on the live horse

The following exercises serve as a guideline:

> Mounting into the straddle seat and side seat,
>
> Clapping the legs together above the horse's back,
>
> Scissors forward and back,
>
> Jumping over the horse from the inside and outside,
>
> Kneeling and standing on the horse.

For the last exercise, one uses an auxiliary rein that is fastened to the girth with both ends.

85. First Instruction with the Goal of Developing a Seat and the Application of Aids.
(See subparagraph 9-13)

During the first couple of weeks, the recruit must gain balance and confidence on the horse. He must be temporarily allowed to hold on to the mane or the saddle so that he will not lose his confidence by falling off the horse. Using the stirrups in the trot right from the start of schooling also serves this purpose among others.

The process of gaining balance is supported by lightly pressing the inner surfaces of the thighs and the flat knee against the horse. Clamping with the lower legs is not allowed. Initially, a supple seat is achieved by having the recruit sit naturally and only ensuring that he spreads the thighs from the hip joint far apart, slightly turns them to the inside and lets the lower legs and feet hang down.

Then one teaches the foundation of the seat, sitting on the buttocks, with buttocks pushed forward. Thereafter one teaches the correct position of the thigh with a deep knee and only then the position of the lower leg and the posture of the upper body.

86. Common Mistakes during Schooling.

Since the recruit should first of all gain utmost suppleness without taking military form into consideration, one must avoid anything that would lead to stiffness and tension. Therefore it is wrong to attempt to teach the recruit the correct seat during the first couple of weeks.

This goal can only be achieved after some time of schooling and by gradually eliminating individual mistakes. It is just as misguided to let the recruit soon ride in a detachment with distances [between individual riders] since he is still unable to apply the aids properly and will therefore be tempted to pull on the reins. If horses, however, go one behind the other without distances for long periods of time, they get used to this and weak riders will later only be able to ride them with distances [to the next horse] by means of predominant rein aids. It is therefore best to take them into open terrain as soon as possible, where the horses are encouraged to go by moving in a pack, without running into each other and where there is opportunity to solidify the horse's balance by riding across uneven ground.

87. Trot and Cavaletti Work.

Initially, the recruit uses stirrups during trot work. In the process one should attempt to teach him to post the trot as soon as possible, since in doing so he learns to correctly distribute his weight correctly on both halves of the horse's body by springing in the knee and ankle joints, and to supply adjust to the horse's movements by going with the movement. As soon as the recruits have overcome their initial stiffness and have learned to somewhat follow the trot movements— generally not before beginning of week three—one starts to also trot without stirrups in the outdoor arena and in the indoor school, since it is otherwise impossible to achieve the stretched position of the leg. In open terrain, one always trots with stirrups. Cavaletti work helps achieve suppleness and improves the rider's feel. Initially, this work is performed in the working trot—with and without stirrups—and at first with, then without side reins. For this purpose, the side reins must be long enough to allow the horse to stretch the neck.

88. Canter Work.

As soon as possible, one should start practicing the canter with the recruits, since it is easiest to learn to maintain balance and push the buttocks forward in this gait. In contrast to the trot, one starts riding the canter without stirrups immediately. In the beginning, the canter is ridden on a large circle, whereby it is developed from the walk, since the recruit sits most securely at the walk and is already able to influence the horse. As an aid to transition into the canter, it suffices to shift the weight onto the inside seat bone, tap the horse with the inside lower leg while taking back the outside lower leg. One key mistake when cantering are clapping buttocks. The cause for this mistake lies in incorrect contraction of muscles and stiffening of joints, as well as clamping with the knees and lower legs. The riding instructor must therefore ensure that the recruit is completely supple and that the upper body moves well with the horse's movement. The recruit must be instructed how differently right lead and left lead canter feel under the buttocks. After about four weeks the recruit starts cantering with stirrups.

89. The Recruit Starts to Influence the Horse.

(See subparagraphs 14 and. 15)

In order to give the rider—after he has gained a secure seat—a correct idea of the extent to which the horse should go on the bit, the assistant instructor or the older rider grasps the reins closely behind the bit and influences the rein hand of the rider just like a horse would do with normal, meaning light, contact on the bit. Once the rider has been instructed in this manner, he is asked to maintain constant contact between his hand and the horse's mouth.

When the rider has become familiar with the possibilities of the individual aids, he must gain the ability to gradually influence his horse in such a way, that he can maintain and improve the horse's posture—that had so far, only been created by means of side reins—by means of his own influence. It must also be explained to him that a horse that moves with through-ness and in self-carriage does not only make it much easier for the rider to assume the correct seat, but that the horse also will be more responsive to the aids. **Right from the start, one must impress on him [the recruit] that the leg and weight aids play a much more significant role than the rein aids.**

90. Schooling Before the Final Winter Inspection.

Without losing sight of the goal of maintaining suppleness, the riding instructor must put greater emphasis on the exactness of the school figures, mastery of the horse in all situations—also when disobedient—and gradually also on military posture. The rider must be educated to independently correct the horse's mistakes in gait and posture by application of the respective aids.

As the schooling progresses in the spring, the instruction should predominantly occur in open terrain. The fact that the recruit's posture can still be improved in the arena should not lead the instructor to view this aspect as the only goal of schooling. Instead, the focus of the schooling is now rather on maintaining what was learned by practical application and to use these skills in cross-country rides.

The "Special Exercises" now increasingly replace the recruit exercises listed in subparagraph 82. Depending on the weather conditions at the end of March, when the individual schooling is concluded, the level of schooling in those exercises, however, can only be limited. At this point, one should therefore not make high demands in those exercises in open terrain.

91. Riding Instruction during the Schooling of Units.

When the schooling of military units begins, the riders learn how to drive in units with horse—drawn vehicles. For the recruits in rider squadrons, MG squadrons and cavalcades, the requirements in cross-country riding instruction must be raised every week, so that the height of their practical skills is reached at the end of May or the first half of June for the inspection of squadrons etc.

XIII. Enlisted Men in the Second Year of Duty and Non-Commissioned Officers.

92. The Schooling of Enlisted Men

The schooling of enlisted men in their second year of duty and of non-commissioned officers is listed in subparagraphs 96 through 101 (subdivision into detachments).

XIV. Officers.

93. First Lieutenants and Lieutenants Who are Entitled to a Horse.

From the beginning of November until the end of March, all first lieutenants and lieutenants take part in an officer's riding lesson five times per week. The officers ride their officer's service horses during this lesson. Under special circumstances, the commanders can instead assign them individual horses in the second year, as an exception also older horses.

The riding instruction during this officer's riding lesson is in accordance with the schooling plan for horses in the second year.

150

Between the third and eighth service year after their promotion, all officers who are entitled to a horse, ride a young remount or horse in the second year of their unit during one winter.

It is desirable to have officers who are entitled to a horse participate in sports competition. The commanders must support them in that endeavor, supervise the preparations, and must reserve the right to give permission to participate in public tests.

Participation in hunts that are organized in the fall is duty for all officers that are entitled to a horse.

94. First Lieutenants and Lieutenants Who are not Entitled to a Horse.

The commanders must take respective measures for the riding instruction of first lieutenants and lieutenants that are not entitled to a horse.

If they are located at the same garrison as harnessed units of their weapon, the officer's riding lesson for these officers must be conducted several times per week. However, one must not use horses of the infantry cavalcades for this purpose.

It is also desirable that officers that are not entitled to a horse participate in hunts; precondition for participation is, however, that rider and horses are appropriately schooled in riding lessons in open terrain and therefore prepared for the hunts, and that the hunts are designed with view upon the skills of the participants (subparagraph 43).

95. Officers of the Cavalry and Rider Regiments and Rider Artillery Divisions.

If these officers are serving in the troop, they must be schooled beyond the requirements of subparagraph 93 as follows:

First lieutenants and lieutenants ride their second service horses in a second riding lesson or a service horse that is assigned to them especially for that purpose or their own horses. This riding lesson must predominantly be used to increase the rider's skill cross-country, to school jumping, and to develop riding instructors in open terrain.

Since it will not always be possible to conduct both riding lessons every day, it is up to the commanders to ensure that the requirements for the officer's riding education are met by giving respective orders. From time to time it will be necessary to expand one of the two lessons. It is then necessary to cancel the other lesson.

If the officers' corps are located at the same garrison as the other weapons, one must also organize special hunts that provide adequate challenges for the officers' horses and the higher level of schooling of these officers.

During the months of November through March, the commanders must organize several rider exercises in open terrain in the format of hunts, cross-country rides, or riding lessons under their supervision for their entire officer corps.

All officers serving in regiments and divisions participate once yearly in a cross-country ride that is put on by their regiment (division) or by a higher duty station. In this ride, they ride their own horses or officers' horses, in exceptional cases and with the commander's consent also service horses. The following requirements serve as a guideline:

Length: 6 to 12 km
Speed: 1 km in two to three minutes,
10 obstacles, 1 m high, 3 m wide.

The first lieutenants and lieutenants participate once yearly—after the hunts or on the occasion of sports competitions on the drill grounds—in several cross-country races that are to be hosted by the respective unit. For this race, they must be divided into fields according to weight classes and must be prepared by experienced officers.

It is desirable to have officers participate in an equestrian sports discipline by competing in public tests in order to improve the individual's performance. For the riding instructor education, it is especially important to participate in eventing competitions. The participation in races is of special value if the officer himself prepares his horses for the races. Those officers who devote themselves to an equestrian sports discipline must be supported in every way, even in case of eventual setbacks.

152

[This page intentionally left blank]

Part E. Special Provisions.
XV. Subdivision into Rider Detachments.
A. Cavalry.
96.

Detachment	Rider
Young Remounts.	Non-commissioned officers and older enlisted men.
Old Remounts.	Non-commissioned officers and older enlisted men.
A.	Non-commissioned officers and older enlisted men.
B.	Enlisted men in the second service year who are candidates for promotion to non-commissioned officer.
Recr., 1, 2, etc.	Enlisted men in the first service year.
C, D, etc.	Rest of the riders.

Horses	Requirements and Comments
All horses in the first year.	See plan for yourng remounts.
All horses in the second year.	See plan for horses in the second year.
All horses in the third year and horses that need rework.	See plan for horses in the second year.
Well-schooled older horses.	See plan for horses in the second year.
Well-schooled horses.	See plan for recruit division.
Rest of horses.	Depending on the horses' quality, some of the horses can be ridden in the double bridle right from the start. The objective that must be achieved is that an average rider can control the horses in working paces and in working posture (also see subparagraph 53).

B. Artillery and Driving Troop.
97. Light Batteries and Driving Squadrons.

Detachment	Rider
Young remounts.	Non-commissioned officers and older riders.
A.	Non-commissioned officers and older riders.
A1.	Non-commissioned officers and older riders who are to be educated as riding instructors.
Recr. 1, 2, etc.	Enlisted men in the first service year.
C, D, etc.	Rest of the riders.

Horses	Requirements and Comments
All horses in the first and second year that need rework.	See plan for young remounts under consideration of footnotes for draft horses.
All horses in the second year and horses that need rework.	See plan for horses in the second year under consideration of the footnotes for draft horses.
Talented horses in the third year.	See plan for horses in the second year without consideration of the footnotes for draft horses. Regts. commander can order the consolidation of such a detachment within the art. (Driving) detachment under suitable riding instructors.
Well-schooled recruit riding horses.	See plans for recruits.
Rest of the horses. Horses that are not suitable for riding must not be ridden, but instead be worked in harness. Their work will be decided by the chief of the battery etc.	Varies depending on horse quality. Horses can go in double bridle right from the start. The objective that must be achieved is that an average rider can control the horses in working paces and in working posture (subparagraph 53).

98. Heavy Batteries.

Detachment	Rider
Young Remounts.	Non-commissioned officers and older riders.
A.	Non-commissioned officers and older riders.
Recr. 1 etc.	Enlisted men in the second service year.

Footnote for draft horses:
For the heavy draft horses, there is no separation between riding and driving period. One must school as many horses as possible in riding to a level that will make them suitable as saddle horses [going in harness with a saddle]. One must not practice canter and jumping. Instead, the heavy draft horses must be schooled in the following exercises during the first year, and these skills must be later reinforced:

Horses	Requirements and Comments
All riding horses and heavy warmbloods in the first year and such horses in the second year that need rework.	See plan for young remounts under consideration of the footnotes for draft horses. The consolidation in the artillery division can be ordered.
All riding horses and heavy warmbloods in the second year and older horses that need rework.	See plans for horses in the second year under consideration of the footnotes for draft horses. The consolidation in the artillery division can be ordered.
Until December: well-schooled riding horses and heavy warmbloods. Starting in December: heavy draft horses.	Until Decemer: see plan for recruits. Starting in December: schooling on heavy draft horses.

Footnote cont'd.
a.) Obedience to rein and leg aids.   b.) Walk and trot straight ahead in working posture. The working trot for these horses is under 275 steps per minute.   c.) Turns during movement: circles, change of rein on the long diagonal.   d.) Halts, backing.   e.) Turns on the forehand, moving horses laterally by partial turns on the forehand and haunches.

C. Infantry, Signal Corps, and Pioneers.
99. M. B. Kp., J. B. Kp., Ffp. Kp.

Detachment	Rider
A	Non-commissioned officers and older riders.
Recr. 1 and 2	Enlisted men in the first and second service year.
C	Rest of the riders.

Horses	Requirements and Comments
All horses in the second year and horses that need rework.	See plan for forces in the second year under consideration of the footnotes for draft horses.
Well-schooled recruit riding horses.	See plan for recruits.
Rest of the horses. Horses that are not suitable for riding must not be ridden, but instead be worked in harness. Their work is decided by the company chief.	Varies depending on horse quality. Horses can go in double bridle right from the start. The objective that must be achieved is is that an average rider can control the horse in working paces and in working posture (see subparagraph 53).

100. Infantry Cavalcades.

One must divide the infantry cavalcades into detachments in such fashion that the final result of the riding education meets the cavalry requirements at the time of the final winter inspection and at the company inspection in the spring (subparagraphs 91 and 102). Their horses should therefore not be used for any other courses. Of the older enlisted personnel, about half should be schooled according to cavalry detachment B (subparagraph 96).

101. Pioneer Companies.

The riding horses of the pioneer companies must be combined into one detachment within a battalion. The requirements must be individually adjusted to the age and talents of the respective horses.

XVI. Inspections.

102. The Regiment or Division and Battalion that Commanders Must Inspect:

1) All divisions with exception of young remounts between early March and end of April in the arena and (units in harness: or) in open terrain. For these inspections, one should require all riding exercises that have been required according to the schooling plans up to this point;

2) For the cavalry and riding regiments and infantry cavalcades, all riders (riding artillery squadrons, the battery troops and the canon operators), also in the platoons end of May or June in open terrain and possibly on the military training grounds. This inspection must be planned for the same time as the inspections for the other branches of squadrons etc.

During the inspection, one must place special emphasis on the rider exercises (see subparagraph 91).

162

At the same time, one must also inspect:

Young remounts of all weapons, as far as they are schooled in the troop, in the indoor school or in the outdoor arena and in open terrain, pack horses, draft horses in harness training according to the driving regulations of 1935 [...] The young remounts are not inspected in harness training. [...]

During the winter and between inspections 1 and 2, the commander must check the consistency of the rider training and the suitability of the riding instructors by occasionally attending the service activities.

For the riders of the MG squadrons of the cavalry and the rider trains of the infantry, one must also inspect swimming with horses once every year.

Berlin, 08/18/1937
The Army Commander-in-Chief:
Baron von Fritsch

INDEX

Hacking out/riding cross-country, 33, 34, 38, 60, 72, 74, 77, 87, 88-89, 92, 93, 99-100, 101, 116, 136, 144, 150
　　horses with conformation flaws, 87
　　young remounts, 114
　　old remounts (second year), 136
　　recruits, 149, 150
　　officers, 151, 152
Half circle and back to the track, 51, 120
Half-pirouette in walk, 51
Halts, 7, 43, 45, 51, 52, 73, 82, 120, 132
Head of the horse, height of, 42, 101, 102, 103, 119
Hunting, 77-78

Individual performance, improving the, 8-9, 92, 93, 119, 137, 138, 147, 151-152
　　by means of participation in competitions, 151-152
Individual training, 3, 8-9, 77, 92, 93-95, 113, 137, 138, 149
　　when swimming with the horse, 92
Indoor riding school, 3-4, 138, 148, 163
　　use of the - for recruits, 138, 148, 163

Jumping, in general, 60, 62, 71, 74, 123, 135,
　　with recruits, 138, 139, 140, 142-143, 146
　　with young remounts, 105, 106, 108-109, 110-111, 112, 123, 124
　　with old remounts (second year), 136-137
　　on disobedient horses, 71

Knee, 28, 31-35, 43, 44, 48, 67, 73-74, 79, 115, 144-145, 147, 148

Lateral angle, 9
Lateral movement of the horse, 59, 86, 118
Lead horse, 71, 75, 79-80, 123, 124, 139
Leading, showing the horse in hand, 27, 62, 67, 79, 87
　　when jumping in hand, 62, 67, 79, 87
Leg aids, in general, 34, 35, 41, 45, 85, 114, 117, 124, 134
Leg-yielding, 54-56, 124
Loading, 41, 91